UNAKA

WILLIAM M KAUFFMAN

This book is a work of fiction.

Any resemblance to actual people, places or events is circumstantial.

For information see author website:
www.williammkauffman.com

ISBN   979-8-218-02743-8

3

Sylvie

The afternoon sun created a yellowish-red glare through the window as Sammy sat alone on the couch in his living room. The room was filled with the elements of his life: three guitars, a mandolin, a banjo and the bass fiddle his wife used to play. It had been a year since Sylvie had passed away. This happened quickly. One day she was in the garden tending to her vegetables and the next day she was vomiting blood with pain raging through her chest. Stage four lung cancer, this was the diagnosis at the initial visit to the general practitioner. Sylvie had made it a total of six months after that. All of Sammy's friends were amazed at the strength she had shown throughout the whole process.

Sammy picked up his 1954 mahogany Martin guitar and began to pick a tune. He was pretty good with the guitar, but this had not happened overnight. As a young man in California, he had struggled with the guitar. His father had been a television repair man. This meant, as a youngster, there were no music lessons for Sammy. Those were hard times. After attending college on the GI bill and working part-time, he landed a good job at a chain drug store. It was at that time that he was able to afford guitar lessons. He smiled to himself as he listened to the resonant sound of the 1954 Martin. He came into the Martin by luck. A frequenter of the many flea markets in central California, he had happened upon the instrument on a Saturday afternoon at a Bluegrass festival. At first, he didn't know what he had when he picked it up. The bridge needed resetting and the neck was warped. Once he began strumming, he knowingly looked inside the sound hole of the guitar. 1954 D-15 Martin, he knew what to do then. One hundred dollars later he had it in his car driving home to his trailer in the hills outside of Modesto.

After a few skillful tunes, Sammy put down the guitar and stood up. Then he began to cry. Waves of sorrow swept through him. He stumbled to the kitchen, hardly able to see through his tears. He stood near the sink and grabbed a wet Terry cloth to moisten his face. The sobbing subsided and he felt better. He turned to look into the back yard. The strength of the setting sun shone into his eyes making him blink. Julie was tied up in the back. Julie was his black, four-year-old Labrador retriever. Sylvie and Sammy had raised her from a puppy. Julie was the only family Sammy had left. He opened the creaking back door and walked up to Julie, taking her leash from the stake to which she was tied. "There, there, girl," he mumbled softly while stroking Julie's black coat. Julie became excited and jumped on Sammy with her paws on his shoulders. The man threw his arms around his dog and gave her a big hug. Then the two friends walked to the house to get ready for bed.

Sammy had lived 72 years. He was born in London, England and became an American when his father moved his family to Modesto, California. Growing up in Modesto, he adopted the California life-style of his day. He was passionate about justice and helping oth-ers, and he loved music. After five years of work at the drugstore, he married. Kelly was a pretty girl and Sammy, himself, was hand-some. He was forced to cut his shoulder length, light brown hair after college to adapt to the world of corporate pharmaceuticals. The drug store business was a bad fit for a dreamer, but it paid the bills. The managers were forever cutting back on labor and forcing longer hours of overtime on the employees. At the same time, they held a tight rein on salaries and had a habit of cutting back on ben-efits. All of this was done in the name of more profit for the share-holders of the company. Sammy, like most people who worked for the company, was miserable and just getting by. Then came a sudden down-turn in the economy. All of his friends lost their jobs when the store they worked at was closed. Sammy was one of the lucky ones: he had been transferred to a small drug store in the far north of rural California near the Oregon state line. He was moving to Redwood, California.

To Sammy and Kelly, moving from Modesto to Redwood was like being banished from civilization. Both young people had grown up in Modesto and understood nothing else. After many arguments, Kelly left him and filed for divorce. She had no intention of moving to Redwood: not with him, not with anyone. And that was that. Un-til then, Sammy had been happy and he thought that he and Kelly were in love. As he bitterly reflected, he had been the only one in love. So, he did not contest the divorce and moved to Redwood alone.

Fifty years later, he was alone again. He got up one morning late and shuffled to the bathroom of his small house in Georgia. This was where he and Sylvie had chosen to live. She was a southern girl. His hair was long again-shoulder length of wavy gray and silver hair. He had grown a beard to look the rural, southern type. And he was still fairly good looking, that is, for a 72 year-old bachelor. He looked at his blue-gray eyes staring back at him in the mirror and could hardly believe the unhappiness he was living through. Just then, Julie began barking at the front door. She could make an incredible noise when she was riled. He could hear the loud scratching of her claws against the wood as she lunged at the door.

"Howdy neighbor," he heard on the front porch as he slowly opened the door while holding back the angry Julie.

A friendly older woman, still fairly attractive with hazel eyes and auburn shoulder length hair, stood smiling.

"I am from Good Samaritan, the local Christian ministry. My name is Mabel," she replied cheerily. "Can we sit a spell and talk?" She asked politely.

"Sure, Mabel. Come on inside and we can sit here in the living room," he replied.

Sitting demurely on the old couch, Mabel took a quick and knowing review of Sammy and the home in which he lived. Through her years at Good Samaritan, she had been adept at reaching out to lonely widowers and widows.

"We heard about the tragic loss of your fine wife, Sylvie," Mabel said quietly.

She had placed her large oversized purse filled with Bibles and nick nacks beside her.

"Will you pray with me Sammy?" She asked looking at him sweetly.

After a quiet nod of her host's head, the woman began to pray.

"Dear Lord above, look down on us miserable sinners living in a sinning world. Have mercy on the good living amongst so much evil. Keep Sammy's Sylvie in your bosom until the day comes when they can be together as one," she continued.

As Mabel finished the prayer, Sammy, who had never been much for church going, began to feel the compassion in her voice and her manner. He sensed the gentleness of her truly Christian nature, and for the first time since his wife's untimely death, he felt happy. When Mabel had stopped praying, Sammy was looking at her with gratitude in her eyes.

"Would you care for some rhubarb pie?" He asked.

She graciously accepted the pie, and once it was eaten, she excused herself to leave the premises to visit again in a week.

After Sylvie's funeral all Sammy's friends had made their condolences and then left. He went to his home alone, as was natural for a man who had lost his only companion. He had lain on the couch, wordless, staring at the ceiling for hours. Then, as the shadows lengthened and the house became dark and more lonely, he had risen and forced himself to feed Julie from her bowl in the kitchen. Going to the cabinet in the small bathroom, he had angrily thrown away all the prescription medications that he had. After disposing of the medicine, he swore to himself that he would never again accept the services of a medical man.

As day followed day and month followed month, Sammy began awakening later each day. There was little reason to get up he had told himself. Friends from the neighborhood were trying to reach out to him. They would walk Julie and feed her, when he was too tired to do so. They knew better than suggest that he see a doctor of any type. All his musical instruments lay unused on the floor of the living room. Everyone was worried about him.

Laying on the living room couch, Sammy could hear Sylvie vomiting in the bathroom. This was her second month of vincristine and cyclophosphamide, following six weeks on intensive radiation therapy.

Despite the drugs, nausea was a big problem. She looked in on him in the living room after coming out of the bathroom. At 60, she was still pretty, but her face now had a haggard, hardened look. He could tell that she was weary of the therapy.

"How are you honey?" She asked weakly.

"How can I be seen you in such misery, Sylvie?" He whispered.

She let her arms hang limply and the leaned on him as he led her to lay down on the couch in his place.

"Let me play a tune for you," he pleaded, and he then picked up the D-15 and began strumming.

In a low voice, he began singing an old Negro spiritual. Sammy and Sylvie had never been religious in a Christian sense, but they were a very spiritual couple. A silent Buddha statue sat in the corner of the living room. Hearing her husband's voice singing, she began humming along softly with him. Soon, she was fast asleep, resting quietly.

Tonight was a bad time for Sammy. He had nightmares all night and had suddenly awakened at two a.m. in the morning. It was August and without air-conditioning in southern Georgia, the open windows of the house brought in the oppressive heat. The sheets on the bed and his night clothes were wet with his sweat. With her claws scratching the hardwood floor, Julie came in the bedroom and lay on the floor on an old throw rug. His eyes were open and wide, and he felt nervous about the future.

"What really do I have to look forward to at 74," he asked himself.

He had been alone now for two years. Mabel had been coming by regularly and at times she brought a Christian friend with her. That was comforting. His neighbors and friends helped him as much as they could, but they had their own lives to live and their own worries. Despite all the help he had received, the loneliness that he felt was intense and unremitting. Fatigue gradually took control of his consciousness and just before dawn, he fell asleep into the only real comfort that he now had.

"Come here girl," he said, clapping his hands one morning.

Julie bounded joyously toward her master. Sammy grabbed her leash and fastened it to her brown leather collar. He took her outside for a walk. It was late September and the first cool days of Autumn had arrived. Too early for the leaves to turn yet, the oak trees lining the old street on which he lived still were a vibrant green. Down a few blocks he passed a woman in her thirties sitting on the steps of a house with a cigarette in her hand. He smiled toward her, not daring to stop and talk. After two miles he came upon the community garden. He and Sylvie, when she was alive, had been very active community gardeners. His wife had made many friends and was a well-known activist in simple and thrifty living. As expensive as groceries were in the area, her efforts were appreciated, and the local newspaper had interviewed her and written about her efforts. Sammy, however, had always been a loner. Without his wife, he was awkward and socially inept.

After the walk, he sat down in the kitchen to eat corn bread and beans. Food tasted off to him and he no longer enjoyed eating.

"I still have to keep a going," he told himself.

The chest pains he had been having recurred and he had a sensation of a heavy weight pressing down on his chest. Fear and uneasiness possessed him, and his body stiffened with the pain. As had been the custom for months now, the pain subsided and went away. He grabbed the phone and called his good friend, Billy.

Billy was Sammy's only "young" friend. He was 26 and a fourth-year medical student at the Medical College of Georgia in Augusta. Billy answered the phone from his apartment in graduate student housing.

"Billy, I am a very sick man," he said hoarsely into the phone.

"Tell me something, Sammy, that I don't already know," the young man said loudly. "You know, you won't take medicines and you won't see a provider," the medical student exclaimed.

"I know Billy, but it don't do no good. You saw for yourself how much good it did Sylvie," he answered back.

"But this time is different, old man," Billy said. "Your heart problems are not stage four lung cancer," Billy said.

"But what about your old man?" Sammy retorted. "Your father did ever thin he was supposed to and he dropped dead at 55," he explained.

"Don't you want something to hope for, Sammy?" Billy asked. "You know, you aren't dead yet," the medical student concluded.

"I may as well be dead, Billy," Sammy answered. "There ain't nothin left for me now, and you know that as well as I am sittin here a talking at you," he said.

After talking to Billy in Augusta, Sammy fell asleep. Sometime during the night he began to dream. In his dream Sylvie was still alive and husband and wife were still together. Sylvie had never looked more beautiful to him than she was in that dream. She appeared to him as a woman in her 40's, about ten years after they had been married. Her figure was womanly and her face was kind. Her lovely blonde hair fell softly on her shoulders as she looked at him. But then after he saw her and saw that she was healthy, he looked down at his arms. The skin of his arms was spotted with the stigmata of old age. Although Sylvie was young and healthy, he was old and sick.

"Where have we been, Sylvie?" He asked in his dream, for his mind had drawn a blank.

"Oh, honey, I just took you to the doctor and now we are back home," she said as her lip trembled with emotion.

"What did he say?" I cain't remember anything, Sylvie," he pleaded.

"Baby, my baby," she said...It's, it's stage four lung cancer. I am so sorry," and she hung her head and began to weep.

Sitting there before his young wife, Sammy felt a shudder go through his entire body.

He stood up and asked her, "how long do I have?"

Looking up into his face through her tears, she said: "you're as dead as I am lookin at you right now." And then the dream faded away.

Late the next day, Sammy still lay in bed fully dressed, only half awake. Faintly, he thought he heard someone knock at the door. In the back of the house, he could hear Julie growl. With effort, he got up and managed to open the front door. Mabel stood smiling on the porch with her oversized purse. With her, she had brought a friend.

"This here is Cynthia, I am introducin you to Sammy," she said.

Cynthia was younger than Mabel. She looked to be about 35 years old. She was somewhat thin and had an austere, religious air about her. Her face was ghostly white and her straight black hair was tied in the back.

"Please to meet you, Sammy. Mabel has told me so much about you," Cynthia said looking straight into his eyes.

"Please come in and sit a spell," Sammy said with a distracted look in his eyes.

The two Good Samaritan women sat on the couch and Sammy sat across from them in an overstuffed easy chair.

Mabel took charge and began to ask Sammy how he had been feeling and what he had been doing. Sammy replied, hardly know-ing what he was saying. The two women gave their host some literature about Bible lessons being given at the Mission on Sunday mornings. As Sammy listened, his eyes were fixed on the small silver cross that always hung from Mabel's neck. As he looked at the cross, he began to relax under the polite conversation of this friendly visit. He realized that like him, Christ had suffered much for others. While Mabel guided the conversation, her pretty hazel eyes looked intently at her 74 year-old friend.

Quietly, she reached out her hands and said, "Sammy, please give me your hands."

The older man put his hands in hers, and then she quickly took one hand and grabbed Cynthia's small, white hands.

"Cynthia, put your hands on top of ours," Mabel requested.

Then the Christian woman began her parting prayer.

"Dear Lord above, have mercy on the wickedness of this world and those left to live in it. Give comfort to the afflicted and lift up the oppressed. Bring the peace of your only son, Jesus, to the heart of your wounded child Sammy. Amen."

As Mabel and Cynthia rose to leave, Sammy rose with them. Impulsively, Mabel put her arms around him, and they stood together quietly for just a moment. Then, the two women left for their next visit.

With time, the older gentleman, left to live alone for the remainder of his days, came to terms with his fate. Mabel and Cynthia were his lifeline, connecting him to the world of caring and compassion. Friends did all they could within their limitations for Sammy and Julie. In some sense, he was a peace now. But he knew that what he had lost with Sylvie could never be replaced.

Noah

Noah worked at the Red Cross. He had an apartment downtown above the German restaurant. His roommate was Robert. Robert wasn't much to look at. He was thick set and overweight, and he usually wore baggy cotton denims and an oversized cotton shirt over his protruding stomach. He also sported a long beard pulled down into two points: one hairy point on each side of his puffy face. Robert wasn't much for hygiene, but that wasn't a problem since he rarely saw Noah, except in the early morning when he came in from the bars.

At the Red Cross, Noah processed disaster claims. He had an Associates Degree in business from Northeastern Community College. The Red Cross office was located on the west side of town, about five miles from the German restaurant. It was next to a big field of chestnut trees. An investor from Kingsport had purchased the land on which the chestnut trees were located. The trees and the land were snarled in legal action between the developers and the Sierra Club. The long legal battle between them was being played out in the city commission meetings on television.

On the weekends, Noah devoted his time to Marilyn, a Navajo Indian girl who had moved from Arizona to upper east Tennessee. Marilyn had tired of the reservation. In Window Rock, the capital of the Navajo Nation, Marilyn had been searching for a change from Arizona and she found it in books about Appalachia. She had taken a Greyhound bus from Window Rock to east Tennessee. When she stepped off the bus in Johnson City, Marilyn found poverty, but with a wetter twist than the desert. A few months after her arrival she and Noah met at a downtown pool hall and soon they began seeing one another. The people of Tennessee were under the impression that Marilyn was Chinese. She had the tan skin, wide cheek bones and the straight black hair of the local Chinese immigrants.

Noah had just finished typing his report on the Gulf hurricane. He rushed the printed product into his boss's office, placing it gingerly amid a growing pile of paperwork. Sam looked up and frowned: more papers to process, he thought to himself. Not giving his boss,

Sam, a chance to find another project for Friday evening, Noah quickly paced down the hall, gave his off-duty notice to Sarah and headed toward the employee parking lot. The aging green Gremlin barely started, and a puff of smoke exited the tail pipe as he pulled onto State of Franklin Boulevard. Turning right at the stoplight, the car made its way past the rundown strip malls and immigrant groceries of West Market Street.

Soon the Gremlin pulled into the visitor's parking lot at the Veterans Hospital where Marilyn worked as an echocardiography technologist. Noah caught sight of her as she was entering the Emergency Room to take an EKG of a cardiac patient. The nurses went about the crowded room of patients laying moribund and half-clothed on hospital gurneys.

"Where is Mr. Thompson?" Marilyn asked the desk clerk.

He pointed his BIC pen at the west corner of the room. She wheeled her EKG cart over to a bed and taped the leads to the patient's gray-haired chest.

"Atrial flutter," she said to the nurse. Soon Mr. Thompson's bed was surrounded by medical residents, only to be shoved aside the attending ER doctor.

While the ER attending gave orders for anti-arrhythmic drugs, Marilyn detached the EKG leads and wheeled her cart to the exit. Noah met her at the entrance to the waiting room.

"This place is really busy," he exclaimed.

Marilyn smiled. "It's the usual Friday night. I'm off in ten minutes," she cheerfully said, "meet me in the hall."

The green Gremlin with Noah and Marilyn pulled from the VA hospital parking lot onto Sidney Street and soon turned east onto West Market Street heading toward downtown Johnson City. Noah contemplated the series of two-story brick buildings with peeling paint as Marilyn reviewed the progress of East Tennessee State basketball. The BUCs had recently defeated Hiwassee in their usual early season match up. Passing decaying pawn shops and a variety of second-hand stores, Noah's mood brightened. Marilyn was always good for the spirit, he realized. He looked at her attractive face and black eyes. She was upbeat no matter how bad things were. This was a skill she had acquired living amid the destitution of the Rez. Pulling onto a community parking lot at the back of Main Street, they soon made their way to Amigo's, a popular Mexican eatery.

The dining room of Amigo's was half empty. The light was an off-color blue from a variety of wide-screen televisions playing sports. The clientele was largely young at Amigo's: students from the university in their first years of adulthood. Choosing a booth in the corner, Noah and Marilyn sat down and ordered. The food at Amigo's reminded Marilyn of the fare she had eaten on the Rez. There she had eaten largely Navajo tacos and fry bread.

"I haven't seen these many Anglo's before," Marilyn thought." Noah was the first Anglo that she had dated. He contemplated the tightly wound bun on the back of Marilyn's head as she bent over her tacos and Mexican tortillas.

"How are things at your new apartment?" He asked.

"Well," Marilyn began, "my room-mate, Shirley has a thing for the head male barista at Starbucks" she said. "After class she headed over there and copies her class notes on a table up front," she said.

"She better keep her mind on school," Noah warned. "I've seen too many short-lived college careers dead end into marriage," he ex-plained. "You are right on track, Mary," he said to her.

Marilyn was taking nursing courses at the College of Public Health during her off hours from the VA hospital. In between, she saw Noah.

"How are things with your boss, Sam?" Marilyn asked.

"Bad as usual," Noah related. "If he isn't yelling at me, he is in his office contemplating the latest customer complaints," he explained. After dinner, Noah dropped Marilyn off at her apartment on State of

Franklin Boulevard, near the university and drove back to his place. As he opened the door and entered the front room, he noticed a pan of burning chili on the stove. He walked over and turned off the burner to keep down the smoke in the room. Robert was asleep in one of the two beds in the apartment. Robert's night stick and bottle of whiskey were on the dresser.

"What are you doing?" Noah said as he pulled Robert off the bed by the shirt. "You are going to burn this place down," he said.

Robert stood up and sniffed, "so what man...Keep off my case or I'll go upside your head with my stick," he said loudly.

"Hey, joker...Eat this stuff!" Noah emphasized and then emptied the smoking chili into a white bowl and then sat it down on the counter. Noah then retreated into the next room to think.

He sat down in a wicker chair by his desk. "The joker can be trouble," he thought.

Robert was about 250 pounds: much too heavy to be dispatched easily if he got out-of-hand. He was a few years Noah's senior and had been in the Army in Desert Storm. He was being seen at the VA clinic, but Noah knew little else about him. Noah had seen reports on television about war veterans going berserk and shooting people.

"Better not rile him," he thought.

He turned the wicker chair at an angle toward a tall window by the desk and opened it to the night air. The room began to clear of the smoke and the smell of burnt chili. He looked down into the street below and saw a few cars drive by.

Noah awoke at four a.m. The portable TV in the corner by the joker's bed was blank with static. He lay awake for awhile and then decided to get up. He showered and shaved, and put on a pair of khaki pants and a long-sleeved shirt. Then he pulled on his jacket. Descending the stairs from his apartment to the street, he decided to go for a walk. Downtown was largely deserted at night. He passed a few homeless men sleeping on the asphalt behind the Energy Gym. The police would pick them up each week and for a few days the spot behind the Energy Gym was clear. Eventually, they all came back. Noah liked to walk the empty streets of downtown Johnson City. He knew it was pretty safe compared to any large American city. Johnson City only had a population of about 60,000 people even when the university was in session. It didn't take much effort for the police to keep local crime under control, and it was rare for anyone to be killed in the fights that occurred outside of the bars. Downtown consisted of about ten blocks of once abandoned, nineteenth century buildings. Some of the buildings were partially renovated and occupied by businesses requiring cheap rent. The German restaurant above which Noah and Robert lived had been in business for about fifteen years. Noah felt relaxed after an hour's walk in the Autumn air. Then he climbed the stairs back up into his apartment. He undressed and fell asleep in his bed.

The current year had been a bad one for the United States with wildfires in northern California, followed by mudslides in southern California. And then there were the hurricanes in Florida and the Gulf Coast. The Red Cross had been busy. Donations had been slacking in the past six months, so the budget of the organization had been under stress with a shortfall of the needed funds. FEMA had been taking a beating on the nightly news, since they never could seem to do enough. Only two people at the Johnson City Red Cross had access to the bank accounts at the local office: Sam and Noah. Locally, the situation with the news outlets had been well under control.

Sam was the manager of the Johnson City office. He was a 58 year-old married man with poor judgment. Partially bald and with red hair in a crew cut style, he had put on about 20 pounds in recent years. Boredom had entered his marriage. His wife, Wanda, ignored him. She was largely involved with the ladies in her church group and was often not at home on the weekends. Their two boys, now grown, had preoccupied her energies in earlier times. Philip was in Atlanta and Reggie was living in Nashville. Like many middle-aged men, Sam had a roving eye. His attention had settled on Sarah, the office administrative assistant. Sarah was a 31 year-old single mother of two boys, ages eight and ten. She had suffered from Sam's stares for years. He had made no attempt to hide the fact that when he looked at her he liked what he saw alot. With his usual lack of reserve, he had let Sarah know that he wanted to see her after hours. She had rebuffed these advances only to have Sam become belligerent and offensive. Finally at her wits end, she had filed a sexual harassment complaint with the Red Cross Regional Office in Charlotte.

"Get this done by four o'clock!" Sam snapped. Sarah shuddered as she recognized his voice. Not daring to look him in the face, she glanced to her side only to be confronted with his generous stomach stretched tightly against the lower portion of a white, button-down shirt. Without answering, she picked up the heavy load of papers to begin working. Sam strode to the front of her desk and placed himself squarely in front of her gaze. Out of the corners of her partially lowered eyes, she could see him staring at her. He needed recognition. She slowly raised her face and said, "yes, sir." Having gotten a response from her, he left and walked into his office, slamming the door shut.

With Sam gone, Sarah relaxed and began to type. On the corner of her desk the radio kept her informed of the local news and entertained her with its "oldies" music. As the office administrative assistant, who did all of the typing, Sarah was aware of all the office secrets. There had been financial irregularities. The budget had not been in balance for years. There had been disciplinary actions against some of the employees. She had typed all the official letters which were delivered to the people under fire by management. The atmosphere at the Red Cross was definitely dysfunctional.

In the back of Noah's mind he heard a fierce noise. It was like the bass drum of a punk rock band, and it came and went, sometimes softening and other times pounding into his consciousness. He turned over in bed to stifle the sound. Dark pervaded the room. He was alone. The pounding began again. He turned his face to the door. There was a shadow moving. The noise was in the next room. He fought himself awake and sat on the side of the bed, throwing off his blanket. Whatever was going on in the other room, he was going to investigate. Cautiously, he pushed back the door. He saw the joker wearing only blue jeans; his bare chest and fat stomach reflected the light of the solitary light bulb hanging from the ceiling. With his night stick in his hand, the joker moaned and began to sob. The joker saw Noah partially hidden in the shadow of the door, and he rushed Noah with the short club. Noah blocked the club, wrenched it free and then, swung it toward the joker's legs, crushing both knee caps. The big man wavered and then fell.

The strobe light of a squad car flashed against the brick side of the German restaurant as Noah began giving his report to the officer. He gave a full and detailed account of the scene in the apartment with the joker. The Emergency Medical Technician arrived as the report was concluding. Robert was strapped down and sedated in the ambulance. The VA Emergency Room was about three miles from downtown and soon the ambulance arrived with its patient. The mental health provider and the orthopedic surgeon on-call were waiting as Robert was transferred inside. Within two hours Robert's knee caps were wired back together. After a few days in post-op, he was taken to the lock-down unit of the Psychiatric Ward.

Back in his apartment, Noah sat, shaken. Despite the odd hour, he fumbled with his cell phone and called Marilyn. Within 20 minutes there was a knock at the door. As he opened the door, Marilyn looked up at him. She had a worried, questioning look in her eyes. Then, she rushed forward to embrace him. They walked into the room where the joker had been. There were large depressions in the sheet rock of the walls.

Sam sat at his desk after the evening staff had left. The janitors had finished cleaning up about 20 minutes ago. He logged onto his computer. Under the customer website of the County Court Clerk office, he entered an automobile license plate number. An address was displayed: 3500 South Roan Street, Washington County. He copied the address down on a three by five card. The heels of his shoes struck the hard linoleum floor as he left the building. The sound of his shoes could be heard up and down the corridor as he left, but no one was listening. Exiting the building, he started his car and pulled out of the parking lot onto State of Franklin Boulevard.

After 45 minutes, he was heading south on Roan Street. His white

Chevy Impala passed Kim's Korean Grocery and a Cuban Restaurant. The car climbed the shallow incline near the Old Castle Clinic. He then passed Burger King at the top of the hill and proceeded out of town into the county. He stopped and turned the engine off on the side of South Roan Street. The air in the Impala felt chilly. It began to rain lightly and periodically he would turn on the windshield wipers. Three houses down from the car was a small wood frame house. There was a large picture window at the front of the house. He could see the outline of a seated woman behind drawn curtains of the window. After he had watched the woman for about an hour, she stood up and left the room. Soon the lights in the house were turned off.

Sam started his car and began heading back north on South Roan Street toward town. It was well after ten p.m. Ashes from his cigarette dropped onto his lap and while reaching to brush the ashes away, his car swerved suddenly. Soon, an unmarked car pulled behind him and began following him. A blue light from the unmarked car began to flash and Sam pulled the Impala over onto the shoulder of the street. A strong flashlight penetrated his driver side window and he heard a loud voice.

"Could you please open the window and show me your driver's license," the voice said. "Step out of the car please," soon followed.

As Sam opened the car door to get out, the officer noticed a brown glass bottle between the two front seats.

"May I have the bottle?" The officer asked.

The policeman took the bottle and inspected it. Then he gave Sam a machine to blow into and asked him to walk a straight line and point to his nose with the finger of one hand.

The next morning Noah was in his office when he picked up an incoming phone call.

"Hey, this is Sam," a voice said. "I'm taking the next two weeks off. Could you put in a leave request for me? I'll see you when I am back from Myrtle Beach," Sam said.

"Okay, boss," Noah replied. "Fourteen days without him will be great," he said to himself as he walked to the front to have Sarah put in the leave request. After two weeks, Sam returned and the atmosphere in the office became troubled again. The natural disasters of Autumn had given way to Winter. Although the boss was back watching everyone, things around the Red Cross were quiet. It was time for the employees to regroup. As always, the year-end financial review was due. Everyone was looking forward to Christmas and New Years.

The accountant had been in the office doing the financial audit for a week. It was now just a few days before Christmas. Sarah and some of the girls had decorated the office with tinsel. There were brightly colored Christmas ornaments hanging from the ceiling. Candy and holiday nuts were placed in baskets on tables in the break room. The buzzer in Noah's office rang. Sam asked him if he would come to the front office.

Noah walked leisurely back to Sam's office. His mind wandered over the events of the past year and his plans for the New Year. As he entered the office, he noticed that the accountant was sitting at the desk with Sam. The review of the audit began. Noah's mind wandered. A $20,000 deficit was mentioned. Sam's face was red, and he appeared uneasy and nervous. The boss's finger was directed at Noah and pointing in the air. There were angry recriminations from Sam. Suddenly, the boss and the accountant stood up and walked toward the door where Noah sat. As he passed Noah, Sam shoved an envelope into his hand.

Noah made his way back to his office and sat down to open the envelope. As he opened it, he felt sick and weak. His mind spun out of control, like a top whirling without direction. He didn't understand anything that was happening to him. He put the pink slip from the envelope quietly onto the desk and began collecting his belongings, placing them into a plastic bag. Slowly, and without talking to anyone, he made his way out of the office to the rear of the building. Once in his car, he called Marilyn and asked her to meet him downtown at the Willow Tree. He told her what had just happened to him. She eagerly agreed to meet him. It was quitting time at the

VA and she was off over the next two weeks for the holidays.

As Noah walked into the Willow Tree, he saw Marilyn sitting at a table in front of the band stand. He approached her and she stood up and grabbed his face with both hands and gave him a kiss. He smiled sheepishly and they sat down together. Although the evening was still early, a rather large crowd began to gather. A rock band from Asheville was scheduled to play. After arriving, the band began to warm up. It was comprised of a delicate-looking female lead singer, two lanky male guitarists and a Hispanic drummer. Gradually, the music became loud and the young men and women began to dance.

"The band is good," Marilyn exclaimed.

Noah nodded, not feeling like talking. The lead singer was talented with expressive phrasings of the lyrics to the songs. After the first set, Shirley, Marilyn's roommate arrived with a date. They quickly sat down. Shirley's date was tall and good-looking with short black hair and square shoulders.

"How's it going?" The date asked and reached over to shake Noah's hand.

"Great," Noah replied.

"How about those BUCS?" The date asked

Noah grinned without answering. The BUCS had a winning season so far, but the majority of the Southern Conference games had yet to be played. The two young men watched the band as Marilyn and Shirley talked eagerly.

In time, Marilyn said she wanted to leave. Noah paid the bill. Shirley and her date left. As Noah walked Marilyn to her car, she squeezed his hand and leaned dependently on him. Turning at her car to say good-bye Noah looked down at her lovely face and almond-shaped, black eyes. He felt strong and self assured.

"I am very lucky," he realized.

Mickey

Sissie and Nannie were trying on clothes in their Mammy's bedroom. Mammy lay silently in a large steel bed. Sissie had told Mickey to sit quietly and play with his toy gun. Mickey sat in the corner. He could see his young mother and his aunt across the room.

"Sisseeeeee..." Mammy suddenly said loudly into the cold air of the room.

Sissie ignored Mammy.

Nannie laughed, "ken you get into this?" She asked cheerily holding up an elegant girdle that she purchased the week before at Sears.

"Nannie honey, you know I don't need it. My figure is still as it was when I was sixteen," Sissie answered.

"Sisseeeee," Mammy reiterated.

"Here Mammy, let me help you some," her daughter said soothingly as she walked over to the bed.

Sissie began straightening her mother's nightgown and took a moist cloth and wiped Mammy's forehead.

"I think she needs to be turned honey," Nannie said looking at the elderly woman's bent and thin frame.

Together, the two sisters tugged at the flat sheet under their mother, deftly turning Mammy onto her other side.

Mickey aimed a shiny pistol at his aunt Nannie. He pointed the pistol at his aunt and pulled the trigger, producing a loud "click."

"He's such a funny chil. What in the worl is wrong with that youngin?" Nannie asked Sissie.

"Hush Nannie, he might be able to hear you," Sissie said with worry.

"But he's over three-year-ol an ain't said nuthin," Nannie pleaded.

"Honey, he may be simple, that's whut his father thinks, but he still might have feelins," her sister replied.

Suddenly, Mickey threw the pistol on the floor and began banging his head on the warped wooden floor. His mother quickly walked over and picked up the three-year-old and sat down in her Mammy's old rocker.

"Baby, don't that hurt none?" She asked quietly as she kissed him on the cheek.

Mickey lay back in his mother's lap with his arms hanging in the air. Sissie had one arm under his legs and one arm cradling his neck and head.

"That's jus sweet honey," Nannie exclaimed, smiling at her sister and nephew. "Mickey, looky here at yer aunt, Nannie ordered reaching down into the large pocket on the side of her gown.

She quickly retrieved a Hershey's bar and held it in the air in front of Mickey's face. Her smile widened and the little boy's eyes opened as she unwrapped the chocolate. Nannie broke off a big piece of the chocolate and put it into her mouth, chewing noisily.

"Oh, yummy Mickey dear, this is sooo good," she said.

Mickey struggled from Sissie's grasp and ran over pulling on Nannie's gown with one hand. With the other hand he pointed at the chocolate bar, held just beyond his reach.

"Here baby, you can have it all," Nannie said with delight as she let Mickey grab the bar away.

Soon, the Hershey's chocolate was history in Mammy's house.

Leaving Mammy and Mickey alone, the two sisters walked back to the kitchen to prepare dinner. Nannie opened a cabinet above the gas stove and rummaged about.

"Here they are," she said as she brought down two cans of creamed corn and a jar of pickled beets.

"Nannie, I need to go out to the Buick and bring in a few things," Sissie related.

Soon she returned with two paper bags filled to the tops with food. She set the bags on the kitchen table and then she moved the two bags to the corner of the kitchen counter. Within time, a pound of lean ground sirloin was frying in a large skillet. Sissie turned over the lumps of ground beef with a large metal spoon as it sizzled in the pan. Steam from the cooking meat rose in the air.

While Sissie manned the skillet, Nannie began chopping up several large cooking apples.

Then Nannie looked up and spoke: "Louis, he ain't happy with all the work it takes to care for Mammy, " she said.

Sissie looked down and frowned. "Men, they cain't understand a daughter's love for her mammy," she related.

"You know, I think the only thing my man really cares about is his wire pen full of short-hair pointers," Nannie said with exasperation.

"Really honey, how much can a bag of dead quail mean when yer wife's mammy is sick?" Sissie asked.

'How is Olen a doin with all the time yer spendin here?" Nannie asked Sissie.

"I think if that man had to say two words to me in one day, he might drop dead," she answered.

"I think I'm late this month honey," Nannie said quietly.

"Oh honey, I know you have so wanted a chil. I so hope it's finally comin to pass," her sister said encouragingly.

All three members of the Storey family were at table.

"Mickey dear, sit up straight in yer chair and eat," Sissie pleaded.

Mickey looked straight ahead without answering. In his young, three-year-old life the little boy had nothing to say. Olen and Sissie worried that their son would never be able to say anything.

"I don't know whut's wrong with the boy, Sissie," Olen complained that night while they were eating.

Sissie had prepared "pigs-in-a-blanket," baked beans and scratch biscuits. The man of the house bent over his plate making quick work of the evening's provisions. Sissie picked at her food, while Mickey stirred his baked beans with his fingers. Grabbing a fist full of beans, Mickey shoved them into his mouth.

Sissie spoke up: "Olen...Nannie tol me last Sunday she is over a month late," the young woman emphasized.

"Well, whut did Louis say to that?" He replied.

"Louis ain't said nuthin, cause Nannie is afraid to tell him," Sissie looked down and mumbled.

"Sissie, don't you go get yerself a month late, hear?" Olen said with a frown.

"If I wanna be a month late, you won't know it until you cain't do nuthin about it, honey," Sissie said firmly.

When Olen heard this, he knew he was beaten. He helped himself to another bowl of baked beans and finished his meal in silence.

Mickey peered over the rail of Mammy's bed. The elderly woman was fast asleep with her mouth held slightly open. Mickey could see the pink of Mammy's tongue inside her mouth as she breathed heavily. It was cold in the room. The coal fire in the corner chimney grate was insufficient to heat the large room. Slowly the little boy reached over to Mammy's face and put his index finger into her mouth. The finger touched the hardness of the few teeth that Mammy still had. The rhythm of her breathing made a faint hissing noise. In the corner of the room near to the coal grate, Sissie and Nannie sat with their eyes fixed on one another.

 "Honey, whut has yer man said now that yer three months showin?" Sissie asked.

"He ain't said nuthin, but that I am eatin him outa house and home," her sister said. "Sissie dear, I am so afraid....Cause I am goin to have to begin thinkin about gettin larger dresses," Nannie related.

"Don't he wonder why you cain't have him a touchin you in the way he has in the past?" The younger sister asked.

"Honey, the ony thing Louis has on his mind right now is that ol car he's been a workin on," Nannie complained.

"You and Louis come over for dinner this Saturday night and Olen and I will bring yer man around," Sissie promised touching her sister's arm gently with her hand.

Sissie sat in the afternoon sun with Mickey in her lap.

"Patty cake, patty cake, baker's man," she said cheerfully as she played with Mickey's hands.

She took both of his hands and patted them together. The little boy lay looking up into his mother's eyes. Sissie was a frail young woman, barely 98 pounds. He could see her green eyes and wavy black hair as she played with him. The young mother wanted desperately for her son to learn to talk. Mickey, however, had stubbornly refused to utter even one word. As Sissie played patty cake with Mickey, in the back of her mind she wondered what he was thinking. She knew that he loved her. Whenever she had left him alone with his father, as soon as Mickey heard her car pull into the garage, he was invariably waiting for her at the back door into the house.

"He just don't like me none," her husband had complained one evening. "He just wants his mommy," Olen had confessed.

Sissie finished the game of patty cake and put the boy on his feet in front of her.

"Come help mommy make din din, honey," she said as Mickey followed her into the small kitchen.

Louis and Nannie were due for dinner that night and there was much food to prepare.

Seven o'clock at Sissie and Olen's house found five people seated around the table. Olen and Louis sat close to the stove near the center of the room. Nannie and Sissie sat near the wall with Mickey between them. Nannie reached over and began smoothing Mickey's unruly hair.

"Ain't chillen sweet, Louis dear," Nannie said looking up at her husband.

"Whut's sweet about him?" Louis asked. Mickey grabbed a hand full of fried chicken and threw it on the floor, while his voice was raised into a scream.

"Cain't you do something about that boy?" Olen said gruffly.

"He's just temperamental honey. You wait, he'll quiet down soon," Sissie pleaded.

"I'd settle for some quiet right now. How bout that Louis? What do you say to all this noise?" Olen asked with a frown looking over at his brother-in-law.

"Nannie seems dead set on this kinda misery," Louis said plaintively. "Listen, Olen, how much does he eat?" Louis asked.

"Our food bill has doubled brother. You don't wanna know the rest of it," was the reply.

Sissie then spoke in a shrill voice: "Mickey, he ain't that bad at all, and he is worth ever penny, I'll have you men know," she said.

Then the thin brunette looked over at Nannie and whispered, "yer honey has sumpin she's been a wantin to tell ye Louis."

All four adults became quiet. Even Mickey was not quite so loud. Nannie looked down into her plate and her voice began to shake with emotion.

"It's happnin to me baby. It had to be me someday, Louis," she said.

Louis looked over at his wife. Her lip trembled. Tears collected in her downcast eyes. No one spoke for several moments.

"It's about time Mickey had a cousin," Louis finally said.

"Do you really think so? I thought you wuz gonna be mad," she said.

"Mad, Nannie dear, I am allays mad, but that don't mean nuthin," he answered gently.

Sissie suddenly stood up from her chair. "I have something for

Nannie in the hall closet," and she left the kitchen.

Soon she returned with an arm full of knitted baby clothes, all brightly colored. For weeks, Sissie had been hard at work, alone at night, knitting baby clothes. She had hidden them in the hall closet so they would be a surprise.

"Sissie, you are just wonderful," Nannie blubbered. "Louis, get me another plate of my sister's cookin, I am eatin for two!" She said.

"Yes, Nannie," Louis answered.

He quickly rose, walked to the stove and returned with a large pot. He waited on his wife like hired help and dished food carefully onto her plate. Nannie ate with gusto, shoveling large portions into her mouth and chewing vigorously. As the happy evening came to an end, the four adults stood up to go. Mickey was taken out of his chair and placed on the floor. As they slowly walked to the door, Olen gave Louis a slap on the back, and the two men exchanged a knowing glance. The two sisters hugged and then Louis and Nannie left for their home.

Louis heard sounds coming from the bathroom. Roused from sleep, he looked over at the nightstand clock and groaned.

"Man alive, it's ony two a.m." he said.

Work had become very stressful, and he needed his sleep. A loud retching sound reached his ears as he realized Nannie was up and in the bathroom with the lights on. The young woman's excitement over being pregnant had transitioned into what pregnancy actually was. Her stomach had grown to enormous proportions with bright red stretch marks across her tense abdomen.

"Nannie don't look nuthin like herself," he had realized with alarm.

His once pretty wife was unattractive. Slowly, he got out of bed and approached the bathroom to check on Nannie.

"Honey, whut's the matter?" He asked quietly.

"Whut's the matter?" Nannie shrieked. Then her voice halted and she began to vomit again.

She was on her knees with her head down over the toilet bowl.

"I am freakin miserable, that's whut," she retorted. Then she held her head up and sat back sobbing.

Alarmed, Louis leaned down and tried to put his arms around Nannie.

"Leave me be," she responded.

Not knowing what to do, he let go of her and just stared at the woman.

"When I said for better or worse, I had no idee how bad it can get," he groaned to himself.

By the time Nannie was through vomiting, she no longer had the strength to yell at her beleaguered husband. The patient husband led his wife from the bathroom back to the bedroom and dropped her heavy body onto the mattress.

"Finally she is gettin some sleepin...The woman needs it bad," he thought to himself.

He laid back down by her side to rest, but he was too shaken by what he had witnessed to sleep. Five hours later, thankfully, Nannie was still sleeping peacefully. Louis had remained awake and tense.

Later that morning it was time for Louis to go to work. "Time to get ready for the hell hole," he thought to himself as he got up.

Louis had never lived with a pregnant woman before, and he was scared. He had no idea how strong women were despite their emotional nature. He dialed Sissie. As Sissie answered the phone, Louis was close to tears.

"Sissie, I hate to call you, but Nannie needs you bad. Ken you stay with her today?" He asked.

Always the dutiful sister, Sissie was at Louis and Nannie's house by the time Louis drove off in his jalopy.

Sissie sat in a stuffed chair in the bedroom as Nannie lay sleeping. Mickey was playing in the living room. The thin brunette had her knitting with her. Not only was knitting creating things for her sister, Nannie, but the rhythmic clicking of the needles was relaxing. Sissie watched intently as her fingers manipulated the needles. The soft yarn wound into something useful. Out of the corner of her eye, Sissie eyed Mickey as he came in from the living room. Nannie's large body lay in a mound with her stomach protruding.

"Louis," Nannie said in a confused voice, "Louis," she said again louder.

Sissie got up and walked over taking Nannie's left hand in hers.

"Yer lover is at work, makin money to bring home to his darlin and his little chil, honey," Sissie explained.

Nannie struggled with her weight and managed to turn her body to the side as her eyes blinked and then opened. She and Mickey were staring straight into each other's eyes.

"Hi baby," Nannie said and managed a smile.

Throughout that day, Sissie carefully watched over her sister. Nannie regained her composure from the night's trouble, arising and taking sustenance about two o'clock in the afternoon. Nannie sat uncomfortably in a wooden chair as she and Sissie visited with each other.

"Sissie dear, has this youngin of yours said anything yet?" Nannie asked.

Sissie's countenance fell. "He ain't said nuthin since I gave birth to him over three year ago," she answered.

Nannie looked over as Mickey sat on the floor playing with his hands.

"He needs friends, honey, and then maybe he'ud talk some," Nannie said.

Standing at the stove, Sissie turned up a burner beneath a pot of vegetable stew. She brushed back a lock of black hair with one hand as she pondered this.

"The little neighbor girl came over, and I caught them two playin together with nary a stitch on," she said.

"Mickey baby, looky here at yer aunt, Nannie said waving both of her hands at the boy.

Mickey put up his left hand and pointed his finger at her.

"No baby, don't point that finger, say sumpin," Nannie said.

Mickey's attention left Nannie and he hopped to his feet and ran to his mother, pulling at her dress while she stood over the stove.

"Mickey, honey, this is fer you," Sissie said as she held a white biscuit before his face. The four-year-old boy stuffed the biscuit down his throat.

The day Sissie took care of Nannie, Sissie's Olen came home to an empty house. His wife had left a note on the kitchen table that she would be at her sister's until late. After reading Sissie's message, Olen looked for something to eat. Sissie had been to Myrick's Grocery a few days prior, and the cupboard provided a variety of foods, predominantly canned goods. Olen emptied a can of Spaghetti-O's into a small aluminum pan and turned the gas burner on. His thoughts reverted back to a time when he and Sissie were young singles. Olen had never been good looking. He was thin and middle height with narrow shoulders. He had mousy brown hair and he had been painfully shy. After class, as a Senior in high school, he worked at Myrick's as a sack out boy. He had seen the lithesome Sissie weekly and had notice her outgoing and winsome nature. All the boys at Myrick's flirted with Sissie except Olen. He stayed near the back of the store and daydreamed. Sissie, herself, had grown tired of the tacky manners of most teenage boys, and she had noticed the quiet boy. She smiled to herself. Many times, she had seen him staring helplessly at her. Growing impatient for the quiet boy to declare his devotion to her, Sissie approached him one morning. Olen looked away as Sissie walked right up to him and stood where he could not avoid her.

With a mischievous look in her eyes, she spoke first: "I think I am a needin help findin the green beans today. Could you lead me there?" She said..

Olen began to panic and started mumbling his reply. He hardly knew where he was as he led the dark-headed, green-eyed beauty back to the produce aisle. And that was how Olen met his future wife. Sissie did not give up easily, and she kept approaching him and asking for help until conversation ensued, and after a much too long of a time, Olen asked her out.

Sissie and Olen by this time had been married over ten years. Olen was now 30 and was already turning bald. Sissie had made a wise choice in marrying him. Olen was loyalty personified. At 8 o'clock, mother and child returned home.

"I made fried chicken and mashed potatoes for Nannie and Louis before I left Nannie's house, Olen honey," she said as she sat down in a chair.

Olen put a plate of Spaghetti-O's for Mickey on the table and he prepared pork chops for Sissie.

"I reckon that baby is about to be born, Nannie looks big enough," she concluded.

"How fer along is Nannie, Sissie?" He asked.

Sissie thought for a moment and then spoke as she began chewing the pork chop, "that gal is ready to pop," she said.

"She's gonna need her sister at the hospital when her time comes," Olen reflected.

"It's just a shame Mammy don't know nuthin about her grandkids, honey," Sissie concluded.

"Your Mammy hadn't known nuthin since the stroke these three year," he replied.

"Mammy don't know Mickey and he don't know her," Sissie said dejectedly.

Olen sat down at Sissie's side and took her in his arms. "Yer just the best daughter yer Mammy could have and yer the best sister yer Nannie could have," he said.

Olen and Louis sat alone in the family waiting area of the local hospital. Nannie had been back in Labor and Delivery for over ten hours. Sissie had been sitting at her sister's side throughout the entire ordeal. At fifteen hours, the brunette with the green eyes took a break and came out and sat beside her husband and brother-in-law. Sissie looked bedraggled. Her eyes were bloodshot and her wavy, black hair was pulled back hastily into a pony tail. Her face was flushed. Although Sissie was only 28, Olen could have sworn that Nannie's labor had put several years of age on his wife. Her forehead was impressed with lines of worry.

"Olen, she's tryin with all her might to bring this baby into the world," Sissie said nervously.

"Whut is the problem, Sissie? When you had Mickey, we wuz in and out in half the time Nannie is takin," Olen remarked.

Sissie's face became grave. "The doctor says the baby has a weak heart, and it's not movin like it should," Sissie answered. "Nannie, she got scared and the doctor had to give her sumpin to calm her down," she said. "Olen, I need to speak to you in private," Sissie said.

The worried pair left Louis in the Labor and Delivery waiting room and retreated into the hall. Sissie looked up into her husband's eyes and tried to stifle herself from crying.

"Nannie is goin crazy with this chil. I have never seen her scream and fight so," she told her husband.

Olen frowned, "why don't these damned medical men just take it outa her and give her some peace?" He asked.

"I think Nannie needs to see Louis, honey," Olen insisted.

His wife's voice raised to a high pitch, "no, please Olen, Nannie cain't let Louis see her like this. You men better just stay away, I am a tellin you," she said emphatically.

If there was one thing that Olen knew, it was that Sissie was much wiser and stronger than he.

"Okay, Sissie, let's go back and sit with Louis," he suggested.

As Olen and Sissie sat back down with Louis, Sissie took out her knitting and started to knit frantically.

"This is a goin to be a special sweater that I am a makin fer this baby tonight," she said. "Nannie will cherish it, cause it came into bein the same night as her baby," she continued.

Sissie sat for a long time knitting. Her husband concluded that she wanted to finish the sweater that night. Olen began to feel nervous. They hadn't heard anything from the doctors.

Louis suddenly put his hand on Olen's shoulder and said: "I'm not sittin here another minute. I am goin back to hear whut the doctors say about Nannie and this baby," he said.

Hearing this, Sissie stood up in Louis' way, but just as she did, a tall man in a white coat approached.

Three months passed. Nannie had given birth to a baby girl, who had struggled to come into this world. Three days post-delivery, Louis took his small family to their depression-era bungalow. Like pregnancy, the young parents soon found out that children are wonderful, but the wonder can wear thin. Louis was awakened at midnight one night by the baby's cries. The house was dark and the temperature in the air was cold. Like clockwork , when little Martha was hungry, she became very angry. And little Martha was hungry day and night. Louis's eyes opened to the loud crying and he looked over at Nannie. She lay on her side with her face turned away from him. All he could see was her blonde hair pulled back around her oval head. He had learned the hard way to do all the feeding at night himself. By evening time Nannie was exhausted and out-of-sorts.

"When little Martha is upset, I don't need the same treatment from my Nannie," Louis thought bitterly.

He clenched his teeth and quietly arose from bed, careful not to wake the sleeping Nannie. The uneven boards of the floor creaked slightly as he trudged to the kitchen. Retrieving a bottle of formula from the ice box, he put it into the bottle warmer. In time, Martha began to feed eagerly as Louis held her. Louis relaxed. Now that all the noise was over, he knew his wife would not be awakened. The warmth of fatherhood filled him as he rocked the baby in his arms. Soon, when the bottle was empty, the little girl fell fast asleep and Louis carefully placed Martha back in her baby crib. Fifteen minutes later, both father and daughter were fast asleep.

Six months later, the two young families were spending an enjoyable evening at Sissie and Olen's home. By this time, Mickey was every bit of four years old. Mickey's parents were feeling glum that night as they watched the mute boy play happily before them. Sissie, despite all her efforts to control herself, started to weep loudly. Olen, Louis, and Nannie felt embarrassed at Sissie's emotionalism. Inside, they all knew how dearly Sissie loved her son. Olen put his arm around Sissie and looked angrily at Mickey.

"Mickey, boy, ain't you got nuthin to say to this wonderful mother of yorn?" He asked the boy.

Mickey walked over to Sissy as she held her head in her hands and finished relieving herself of her maternal suffering. The little boy put his left hand out and patted Sissie's hand.

"Don't cry mommy," he then said.

Sissie's head jerked upright.

"Whut...whut did you say, Mickey?" She stuttered.

"Don't cry mommy," Mickey again reiterated.

The young mother gathered the boy into her arms eagerly.

"Did ever one hear this?" She asked loudly. "My Mickey can talk... This youngin is a talkin," she said.

No one was more surprised by the talking child that night than his father.

"I cain't believe it Mickey," he said as he looked down at the boy. All this time you have been a torturing yer parents with no talkin, and you coulda talked whenever you wanted," he said to Mickey.

No one in Mickey's family ever discovered why the boy, who for four years would not talk, really could have talked anytime he had a mind to. They all pondered the mystery. Not only could the boy speak words, but he knew sentences and talking like any other four-year-old in the neighborhood.

Mary and Ruby

Ruby worked in the silence of the early morning. Sunrise had just occurred, but the remainder of the night cast a shadow in the corner of the living room where she was at work. At this time of the year, during the Winter, the sun would not rise much. Rather, it moved in a circle, staying low near the horizon. Ruby's fingers were stiff with cold as she cataloged her papers. Stacks of papers were neatly arrayed around the walls of the rectangular living room. Forty-two years ago, as a young woman, she had studied with a local mystic in the small southern town in which they lived. He had taught her much, and she missed the close companionship of their years of study.

A faint sound issued from the adjoining bedroom, where her crippled sister, Mary, lay. Ruby rose from her cane chair and made her way to check on her sister. Laying on her side, Mary's half-opened eyes showed the mature, white cataracts that had left her blind.

"Mayree deah," Ruby whispered. "I know you will like hot cream-of-wheat this mornin," she said.

The crippled woman turned onto her back with her face toward the voice in the room.

"Please Ruby, you're such a deah," she replied with a sweet smile on her lips.

Mary had been crippled with polio since childhood. Ruby could not remember a time in which her sister had not been in a wheelchair. Forced to live a sedentary life, Mary had been an avid reader. With old age and the onset of cataracts, her reading had ended. Still, her mind remained alert, despite the limitations of her disabled body. Mary had lived with her parents, Rosco and Sally Biggs until Ruby had been abandoned by her husband of three years. Soon thereafter, Ruby had taken Mary into her home, and the two sisters spent their lives together. They sat at the gray micra table in the kitchen as cream-of-wheat boiled on the gas range. The steam from the boiling water gave the room a warm, cozy feeling. On a shelf over the range, a small black radio gave the morning's news.

"Harvey Dodson, Paducah Police Chief, reported to WDXR that Mark Sumner escaped last night from the Eddyville State Penitentiary. The convicted killer of the Ritz Hotel heiress, Viola Duncan, has been at large now in the Jackson Purchase for over six hours. Witnesses outside Wayne's Country Kitchen near Littleville reported the theft of a 1931 green Chrysler in the early morning hours...And now for the weather," the radio sputtered.

Ruby switched the radio to a local country station and the two women ate in silence as the latest songs from the Opry in Nashville played.

"Reckon the ice in the river is ready for cuttin?" Mary asked.

"I'll go over to Haws grocery and check at noon," Ruby replied. "This ol ice box could use a fresh supply." She said.

Later that morning, after Mary was dressed, she sat in front of a bureau mirror flecked with the effects of many years. Ruby had taken down her sister's hair and stood behind her with an ivory-handled brush performing a daily ritual. Mary sat in the wheelchair facing the mirror as her long white hair was being brushed. Ruby reflected on the many years since her younger sister had come to live with her. After her husband left her, the young Ruby applied for a job as a typist at the Illinois Central Railroad shops. The railroad was the largest employer in Paducah at that time. She had been recommended by her sister, Elvira, who owned a beauty shop near the Illinois Central. In high school Ruby had taken secretarial classes and she was a proficient typist. Mary, who was sixteen years old at the time, was able enough to manage around the house alone without her older sister. In the evenings the two single women had the company of Mr. Abe Langston, who visited them to continue his studies in Eastern Religions. Ruby, having married at age 20, had no college education, but she was bookish and intelligent.

A firm hand knocked at 1301 Monroe Street. A 23-year-old woman rose from her stuffed chair and opened the wooden door.

"Evening Ruby Mae," a tall man in his 50's stood displaying a friendliness particular to the South.

"I have just discovered an English translation of Pantanjali's Sutra," the woman said quickly.

Middle height, with a round, plump face and auburn hair pulled back into a bun, Ruby Washburn was typical of many women in Paducah. In the back of the room in a wheelchair, her sister sat with a volume of English poetry opened on her lap. Mary did not look up nor acknowledge the gentlemen visitor.

"I can see that you have been to Readmore Used Books, Ruby," he said with excitement. "Readmore gets their pick from the libraries of the estate sales," the man reflected.

"Please sit here with me Mr. Langston," Ruby said as she pulled two chairs up to a long library-style table standing against the wall.

Already laid out on the table was the copy of the sutra, along with a dozen dusty volumes of Hindu and Buddhist writings.

The mantle clock chimed slowly ten times. "I do believe it's already ten o'clock," Abe Langston exclaimed.

He took his round, wire-rimmed glasses from his eyes and looked over at Ruby as she sat nearby contemplating her reading.

"I have something I made special for you to take home, Mr. Langston," his study partner mentioned as she got out of her chair and looked at the clock. "I'll be right back, you just sit here a spell longer," Ruby pleaded.

Retreating to the kitchen at the back of the house, she soon returned with a small, covered basket.

"I know you like my fried apple pies, and these pies are fresh from this mornin," she said as she handed the basket to Abe.

"I'll be, well if that ain't my fav'rit," he said with pleasure.

"Don't mind Mary sleepin in the corner. I'll let you out," Ruby said.

Abe gave Ruby a familiar peck as she turned her cheek slightly up for the usual good-bye.

"Next Tuesday is good for me, how about you Ruby?" He asked as she opened the door.

"Tuesday it is, Mr. Langston," she replied, and they parted.

Years later, Ruby and Mary sat in their living room in the late afternoon. Ruby had never been focused on housekeeping. The dishes from the day's breakfast and lunch remained unwashed in the kitchen sink. The dust from the house could be seen floating in the air, highlighted by the afternoon sun that found its way through the tall, narrow windows of the house. As usual, Ruby was bent over her latest book. Mary, crippled and blind, fingered her loose white hair with a withered hand.

"Honey, this here is a sad ol world," Mary said at once.

"Well, Mary dear, we are still havin whut our President says is a bad economic depression," her sister said beneath her breath.

"Sister, I thank the Lord I don't have the eyes to see the kinda misery a goin on in this ol town," Mary said.

"Yes, dear, there is something to be said for not havin to look at whut can only be described as ugly," Ruby replied.

"How long has it been since your Abe Langston passed, honey?" Her sister asked.

Ruby felt a twinge of sadness and then answered, "It's been a very long while, but I can remember ever thing the dear old soul taught me," she said.

"How's that, Ruby?" Mary asked.

"Well, the Buddha taught us to free our minds from the sins and cryin of the painful world around us. Once y'all can do that, then you'll fill yourself with the beauty of your own thoughts," she said.

"He was so wise, warn't he?" Mary asked Ruby.

"Yes, that man was wisdom itself," her older sister concluded.

As Mary and Ruby discussed the past, the Great Depression was going on outside their door. Unemployment lines and soup kitchens dominated every town in the country. The world seem cold and bleak to most people, including the people of Western Kentucky. People struggled to maintain even a threadbare existence. Hobo towns had sprung up around the railroad cars at the local Illinois Central Railroad Shops, from which Ruby had fortunately retired. As the two elderly women sat in silence, a police siren wailed in the distance. Ruby sat with her hands folded over her round stomach and Mary continued to finger the strands of her long hair.

"Are you happy?" Ruby asked Mary.

"Sometimes, but not especially now," Mary answered slowly.

"Would you like to be happy, honey?" The question was put to her.

Mary didn't answer. After a long period of contemplation, Ruby stood up.

"Let's invite Sissie and the young'uns over for Sunday dinner," she said.

If Mary's blind eyes could have twinkled, they would have twinkled right then.

The Illinois Central Railroad, connecting Cairo to Galena was begun well before the War between the North and the South. During the time of Ruby and Mary, the lines of the railroad connected New

Orleans to Chicago. The activity of the Shops in Paducah, Kentucky was the economic lifeline of that small southern town. Young Ruby, young Mary, and the middle-aged Abe sat in Ruby's living room after an active evening of study. The gentleman looked into the distance of the room as he smoked his pipe.

Then Abe beg to speak. "Yes, ladies, I just got off the IC Central in Chicago when them big riots broke out last week. The union men, they wuz gunned down by the police and it was a darned sorry sight to see," he said.

Ruby spoke up. "The union men they wuz desprit, I'll have you know," she said.

"Desprit or no desprit, ye cain't bomb the police," Abe answered.

"I know yer right," she answered. "Don't the Eastern sutras preach agin violence of all kinds?" Ruby asked.

"Yep, even to the point of not killin yer meat to eat," he reflected.

"No hold on thar," Mary spoke from her corner. "Ain't no one gonna take fried chikin away," she said.

"Mr. Langston, some things we are gonna eat, no matter what the Hindu say," Ruby confirmed.

"I confess, I have eaten animal flesh myself at times," Mr. Langston related.

"That some kinda funny Hindu we are here, don't you say," Ruby acknowledged.

As Abe stood and made his excuses to leave, Ruby ran to the kitchen and came back with a bag and pushed it into Abe's hands.

"Here's some of that evil chickin to take away with," she said.

Abe kissed her on the cheek and then left.

Saturday morning Ruby awoke earlier than was her custom. She roused her sister from slumber, fixed breakfast, and placed Mary in her chair in the living room near the large window. Then she put on her long coat, tied a scarf around her head and got her wheeled shopping cart from the hall closet.

At 75, she still was able to walk the seven blocks from her house on Monroe Street to Haws Grocery. Once inside the neighborhood grocery, she went through her list for Sunday dinner when Sissie, Mickey and Danny were due to arrive from Cornell Street. She needed things that would appeal to two little boys and also be acceptable to their mother. Sissie was Ruby and Mary's grand-niece and she lived on the other side of town. Sissie was married to Olen. Once the wire-framed shopping cart was full with food and the check had been written, Ruby made her way back home with the cold Winter wind following her footsteps.

Sunday morning Mary sat and listened to her sister prepare the meal for later in the day.

"Why don't you make pumpkin pie?" Mary asked.

"You know Danny and Mickey don't like pumpkin pie. I know it's your favorite, but this dinner is for the young'uns." Ruby answered.

"Sister, don't you think it's time to take the ham out of the oven?" The woman in the wheelchair retorted.

"Now how many time have I told you, Mary, that when it comes to cookin, I am the boss here," Ruby said almost starting to become angry.

"I reckon Sissie don't think so after you burned the biscuits last month," Mary answered.

At this point, the cook stopped talking and began ignoring the commentary from across the room. The truth was that Ruby was a terrible cook, but Sissie was too well-mannered to bring up the point with her. In due time the meal was prepared, and Ruby placed the dishes for five around the table.

"Danny, you sit up young man and eat three mouthfuls of ever thin on yer place," Sissie demanded as the meal began.

The young mother then began spooning green peas and onions onto Mickey's plate. Mickey was five years old and his brother, Danny, was eight. Mickey began picking up the onions with his hands and looking very closely at them.

"Put that down and use yer spoon!" Sissie shouted.

Ruby and Mary smiled. They were used to the spectacle of the two young boys at table. For Sissie, however, dinner at Great Aunt Ruby's was always a struggle. Be that as it may, Ruby and Mary were her favorite relatives.

"Danny and Mickey, you two boys ready for a fried apple pie?" Mary asked. "You know yer Great Aunt Ruby made a big batch just yesterday," she said.

"I wanna fried apply pie mommy," Mickey suddenly blurted out.

"Mickey, you eat one more bite of the green peas and you can have one of Ruby's pies," was the mother's reply.

During the dinner with Sissie, Mickey and Danny, Ruby's mood had improved greatly. After company departed, she went about cleaning the used tableware and storing left-over food in the ice box which stood in the corner of the kitchen. Great Aunt Mary had already wheeled herself into the living room, so Ruby was alone. She smiled to herself. The boys were so precious.

"Just what I woulda wanted if'n I had my own," she reflected.

Not having children had been a great sadness for Ruby. After her young husband had left her, she made a firm commitment to remain single. Mary had moved in, and Mary needed her. This was enough to fill the rest of her life. And then there was Abe Langston, while he had been alive. His kind manner to her always satisfied a need for male attention. But then, after Abe died, there was a void in Ruby's life that was never again satisfied. Later that night, she sat alone in the living room. Mary had been sleeping soundly for some time. Her thoughts drifted to Abe and the many years they had studied together.

"I think I can feel Abe with me now," she thought as she sensed a presence in the room.

The only physical sound was the mournful tick tock of the mantle clock.

"Abe alays tol me that when the body dies, the spirit stays," she remembered. "The spirit gets a new body and lives on forever, over and over, until Nirvana," she reflected.

Now, as she recalled the Hindu mantras that she and Abe had stud-ied, she repeated one of them. She thought of the meaning of the Sanskrit words, and she felt her soul merging with the eternal reality of which she and Abe were still a part of. Ruby wondered to herself if anyone she met around town could really be her lost friend in a new life.

"He's somewhere in this town, I know it," she whispered to herself.

Over the next few weeks, after Sissie's visit, Ruby threw herself into her studies. Books had been a great escape from the harsh real-ities of life during the Great Depression. Many of the people she felt closest to, beside family, were people who had lived thousands of years before in another part of the world. In the small southern town in which she and Mary had been born and lived, they had little in common with the local people. Abe had been a wonderful exception to many of the personalities she dealt with in Western Kentucky, but even that had not lasted. Sitting at the long table at which she once sat with her closest gentleman friend, she thumbed through a large volume of religious work.

"Ruby, can I get you to bring me a sweet tea?" Mary asked from the other side of the room in which they both sat.

"Sure honey, I made a big jar this mornin," the elder sister said.

Ruby promptly returned from the kitchen with a tumbler of this local beverage. She carefully held the glass of tea to her sister's lips as Mary satisfied her thirst. The invalid wiped her mouth with a hand.

"Read me something purty, Ruby," she pleaded.

Ruby picked up a volume of the English poet, Shelley, and opened the book. She turned to the "Ode to the West Wind," and began reading in a halting voice. Although her mind was clear, as she entered her eighth decade of life, Ruby's speaking voice had developed a trembling quality. She recited the familiar verses in an otherwise silent room. As her sister finished reading, Mary spoke.

"That war Mammy's favorite, I guess you know, sister," she said.

"Yes honey, she and Pappy loved Shelley," Ruby replied.

"Pappy could never stand to cross Mammy. She ruled over him like a queen," Mary said.

As Ruby was well-aware, the poet Shelley shared many beliefs in common with her departed friend, Abe.

"This fella Shelley, honey," Ruby spoke, "he didn't believe in vilence and he didn't eat no animal flesh." She said.

"But the worl is a vilent place, and there is much to suffer because of it," Mary returned.

Ruby looked at her life's companion. She stood up and walked over to her sister. She began stroking Mary's hair. She pushed her wheelchair companion to the bed in the next room and struggled with Mary's weight as she helped her to lay down for the night. Then, she undressed, put on a sheer nightgown, and lay down.

The Kerley's

Henry stirred his oatmeal while he looked out the window. It was early on a winter morning, just about sunrise. Despite the warm glow of the sun through the window, the outside had a frozen look. There was frost on the dried, brown grass in the yard and there was ice on the branches of the trees. The new family that had moved in across the street from his farm had not begun to stir. There was a father, a mother, and four children. There were three boys and one girl. The family had moved in since the beginning of the new school year in the county. Henry, his wife Eadie and their adult daughter, Becky, had watched the new family come and go in the late summer evenings.

After an hour's reflection, he rose and put ashes on the fire in the chimney to keep in the warmth. He put on his woolen work coat and walked outside toward the barn. Henry was 83 years old. He had spent his entire life farming. Unlike his more modern contemporaries, he had always done his plowing with a mule. He had no need of a tractor. This meant that his annual crop was meager. Still, it was enough to keep his small family with the essentials. As a young farmer, he had a team of draft horses, and he hired teenaged boys from the neighborhood to help him with the plowing. Over the years, the quality of the soil on his land had become depleted, and his land was rutted from erosion and the loss of topsoil. Still, at age 83, he managed to raise most of the food that he, Eadie and Becky ate. Although he now lived off an old-age government pension he still kept one mule.

Henry's breath felt cold in his lungs as he walked to the barn. A thick pair of gloves kept the worst of the chill off his hands as he unhitched the gate to the barn. Inside, the mule stood facing the door, watching the farmer as he entered. The barn was drafty, and the Winter wind easily penetrated the spaces between the boards in the walls. The tin roof was effective in keeping the rain at bay, but it also transmitted intense cold into the structure during the frigid months. Aside from one mule, Henry kept a number of Barred-Rock chickens and a few Mandarin ducks in the barn. He dumped a sack of dried field corn into a bin in the mule's stall and he spread cracked corn around the frozen soil below for the chickens and the ducks. The bird life became lively and hurriedly ran about picking at the cracked corn. Henry used an old hammer to break the ice in the water tank, and he dipped out a bucket of water for his mule. In the back of the barn was the chicken coop. He gathered the night's crop of eggs into the large pockets of his coat and then he walked back to the house.

Back inside the house, he put the eggs into a bowl on the kitchen counter and made his way to the rocking chair facing the front window and the road. Two neighbor children stood near his driveway to wait for the county school bus. They were both boys.

Henry tried to estimate the age of the boys. "I would reckon the older is about ten years and the younger is about six," he thought. "The little one is probably starting first grade at Lone Oak and the older must be about the fourth grade." He estimated.

He could hear the voices of the two boys as they argued, but he was too far away from the road to hear their exact words.

"Education has come a long way," the farmer thought. "In my day, in the early 1900's, you didn't need much schoolin. What you really needed was trainin in farm work," he said to himself. His father had done his best, Henry felt. He had taken Henry out of school in the sixth grade and put him to work on a neighbor's farm.

He looked down at his hands in his lap. His knuckles and fingers were large and the skin of his hands was calloused. As an older man, the joints of his fingers were stiffened by arthritis. His right forefinger had bent into a curve that he could not straighten. Henry could not read nor write. When he made his purchases at the local farm supply store the owner accepted his check with a poorly inscribed "X" in place of his name. When he was still in elementary school, he could read and write. The lack of practice over the years had degraded his skills. Even while he was in school, he received poor marks for penmanship. His effort at writing had been lacking, but like many men his age who were illiterate, he had a prodigious memory. He could recite numerous facts and stories with remarkable accuracy.

Henry felt a hand on his knee. The hand shook his knee back and forth slightly. He woke up and looked at the mantle clock.

"You've been sleeping," Eadie said from the chair just across from him.

He looked at her. Eadie was in her mid-sixties. She had been in her twenties when they had married.

"That was in 1920," he remembered. "Just about two years after the great war in Europe," he thought.

Many of the farm boys his age had been shipped to the fields of France and Belgium to fight the Kaiser. He had been exempted from military service by a bad back and bad feet,

"I don't think I would have been much good at soldiering," he had realized.

But he had not liked being left behind when there was fighting to do. His job, however, was to stay in Western Kentucky.

"I went callin on the family across the road last week," Eadie mentioned to Henry as he roused himself from slumber.

"I think the father works at one of the factories in Paducah," Henry mentioned. "Reed Finley had a talk with him at the Farm Supply last month," he continued.

"Well, his wife is called Ruby Mae," Edie interjected. "She is from a large farmin family in Graves County south of here about 20 miles," she finished.

"How is this Ruby Mae managing with all them youngins?" Her husband asked.

"I don't have to remind you, Henry, that we Kentucky farm wives know how to work," Eadie related. "I sat down in the living room with her, after introducing myself, and we had a nice chat while she knitted a blouse for her little girl, Shawna," she said.

"I spose she is mighty lonely being 20 miles from her folks in Graves County," her husband suggested.

"I reckon that is so, but I am here to see that she don't get too lonely," Eadie conveyed. "She invited me over tomorrow to can Elderberries with her. I gave her all my extra mason jars as she is short," Eadie continued.

"Tell her to give you some of the jelly once it's made," Henry pleaded.

"I know Elderberry jelly is your favorite and I am sure that Ruby Mae will oblige," Eadie promised as she stood to leave her husband.

During World War One, Henry was one of the few men his age left behind. As a young man, he provided day labor for the elder Finley who was Reed Finley's father. Grandpa Finley had the largest farm on Lebanon Church Road, so big that it extended to front the highway to Paducah. In addition, the elder Finley had been a successful horse trader at the local livestock auctions. Before the end of the great war, Henry often frequented the turkey shoots during the holidays, trying his luck against the older men.

"This 22-caliber rifle should do the trick," he had told himself one night in 1917 as the turkey shoot was getting under weigh.

Having hunted quail with his father before the war, Henry had developed a keen eye for small targets. There wasn't much need for rifles, though every man had one. All the men and their sons depended on the 16-gauge shot gun for quail hunting.

It was late Saturday night in November 1917. Things had not gone well for Henry at the turkey shoot. His aim was off, and he hadn't hit a target center all night. At the snack bar having an Orange Crush, sixteen-year-old Eadie Schmitt struck up a conversation with him.

"I noticed your rifle has a fine walnut stock," she mentioned as she looked up from a bag of popcorn.

"Yep, and walnut is hard to find in a 22-caliber rifle in these parts," he replied. "Would you like to hold her, Eadie?" He asked her.

"Let me see that gun, and I'll show you how it's done, if I can borrow her," Eadie suggested.

"Here she is. Give things a try," Henry said as he handed the rifle to the teenage girl.

Eadie, who had bright red hair and freckles, took the rifle knowingly, paid the shooting fee and took her place to shoot. Much to the farmhand's surprise, she was doing surprisingly well against the sharp-shooting of the older men of the area. After 30 minutes, she had placed second in her line, and although she didn't get the turkey, she did get a large portion of barbecue as a prize.

As Henry and Eadie were walking out together, she turned to Henry and said: "this gun is a beauty to shoot."

Henry noticed then just how cute Eadie was, and he had known her all of his life. It was just a matter of time until he called at the Schmitt house and asked Eadie out. Eventually, they tied the knot, and Henry with the help of his father-in-law was able to buy 55 acres of land on Lebanon Church Road.

Eadie stood on the narrow concrete porch at the front of her neighbor's house. After a short time, Mrs. Bone opened the door.

"Come on inside, and don't mind the way things are Mrs. Kerley," Ruby Mae exclaimed. Howard and the boys haven't done their share of the cleanin this week," she said.

"Thanks," Eadie said as she stepped inside the farmhouse. "I think I can smell some of those Elderberries now," she said as the two women walked back to the kitchen.

Ruby Mae was a small woman, about five foot two and one hundred and ten pounds. She was slight for a Kentucky farm wife, most of whom had put on a few pounds after having had their children. Inside the kitchen were a variety of large aluminum pots for boiling the fruit Stacked along the counter and arrayed on the steel and micra table were the glass jars for the berries and pectin. The water in the pots had already been brought to a boil and steam had collected on the inner sides of the glass of the windows.

The two women worked with the fruit while they got to know one another.

"What kinda work does your Howard do, Ruby Mae?" Asked Eadie.

"He's the foreman of the receiving department at Modine Manufacturing in Paducah," the young woman answered.

"How're they treatin the men down there?" The older woman asked.

"Oh, Mrs. Kerley, things ain't good," Ruby Mae complained. "Ford is losing money and new orders for radiators are down," Ruby Mae said.

"I'm sorry to hear it," Eadie said soothingly.

Ruby Mae looked down as she worked the Elderberries through the colander.

With a tremble in her voice she said, "last week Howard grabbed a half-empty can and got acid all over his right hand. Burned half the skin offin that hand," she said.

"I'll send Becky over tonight with a nice jar of cider to help take the pain away after your man gets home," Eadie replied.

"Much obliged," Ruby May said.

After two hours, the fruit had been prepared for the mason jars and the jars were full. The vacuum seal lids were put on and the jars were set to cool. The two women exchanged a hug on the porch of the Bone house and Eadie made her way back to her house.

After Eadie walked home, Ruby Mae began storing the jars of Elderberry jelly on shelves in the basement. The stairs to the basement were narrow and rickety. Lighting in the basement was poor. Back in the kitchen, she began to prepare dinner. Ruby Mae was a gourmet cook, although she had barely finished high school. As the dinner was nearing completion, her two eldest boys began setting the table for supper.

"Denny go get your little sister and put her in her highchair," Ruby Mae pleaded with her black-headed five-year-old.

The little boy dutifully walked back to the back bedroom where Shawna lay on thick blankets playing with a stuffed animal. Once in her highchair, Shawna began crying.

"Mommy, my tummy hurts," the little girl raised her voice.

"Here, try this," Ruby Mae said as she gave Shawna a glass of milk sweetened with honey.

Knocking the glass to the floor and spilling its contents, Shawna raised her voice into a scream. Ruby Mae put her hands to her ears and began to cry. Gathering her strength, she took Shawna from the highchair and sat on the living room couch to comfort the little girl.

At once, the front door opened and Howard appeared with a frown on his face.

"Haven't you done the cleanin today?" He said rudely as Ruby Mae sat on the couch facing him with Shawna in her arms.

Ruby Mae did not answer her husband, but started soothing Shawna's soft brown hair. Howard picked up a shoe from the floor and flung it across the room. Hearing the shoe hit the wall in the corner, Billy, the second eldest boy, appeared through the door to the attic. Standing in the doorway with a whimper on his face, he looked at his father.

"Stop cryin, or I'll give you a real reason to cry!" Howard shouted at the boy

"Billy, go get your brother and we'll all sit down and eat,"Ruby Mae said softly as she turned to Billy.

"Okay, mommy," and Billy scrambled off to find his two other brothers.

At dinner, the little family sat stiffly without talking. Howard was at the head of the table in his "captain's" chair. Before eating, the man of the house asked everyone to bow their head while he recited the evening prayer. On the lamp table in the corner sat the family Bible in its stand.

"Pass the green beans to your brother," Ruby Mae instructed her oldest son, David.

The two younger sons, Billy and Denny, sat opposite one another and the baby, Shawna sat in her highchair.

As the silent eating continued Howard spoke up. "How many times have I told you, Ruby, that I am especially fond of boiled potatoes with the jackets on?" He asked as he looked aside at her.

Ruby looked into her plate and didn't answer. A fine array of vegetables adorned the table, accompanying a large piece of roast meat. For dessert, Ruby Mae had prepared an English tea ring pastry. As the evening meal concluded, Howard retreated to a stuffed chair in the living room. David and Billy cleared the table of its dishes. Ruby took Shawna to the back room to her crib, and the youngest boy, Denny, lay on a rug in the living room in front of the chimney.

The next morning at nine a.m. Ruby Mae sat alone. The bedroom chair in which she sat overlooked a bare hill behind the house. At the top of the hill stood a pair of hickory nut trees with a worn dirt path between them leading over the top of the hill. She looked through the window at the clouds in the cold sky. Howard had been difficult to live with since they had moved to Western Kentucky. But things were much better for her than life in Eastern Virginia. There she had been far away from her many relatives. Since her husband had started working at the radiator factory in Paducah, business in the automotive industry had collapsed.

Ford had drastically cut orders for radiators from the plant in Paducah. To compensate, management laid off workers and those who remained worked longer hours. A five-day work week became a six-day work week and now the men were working seven days per week. Ruby picked up her knitting and began to work the yarn. Knitting relaxed the young wife and her little girl needed clothes. The children's sweaters at the local Sears store where she shopped were expensive, she thought to herself. Like her mother before her, Ruby made all of her own clothes and most of the clothing for her four children. Among the three boys, when a younger boy grew, he took the hand-me-down clothes from the next older boy.

As Ruby sat alone knitting, she began to daydream about how her life might be in years to come.

"If Howard could manage to save up some money, he could buy that little hardware store in Lone Oak," she thought. "That way, he wouldn't have to kow tow to the slave-driving managers at Modine Manufacturing," she told herself.

"Modine is just not a good place to work," Howard had explained to his wife one night. "The union is driving me crazy," he had said to his wife.

Howard was the foreman of the receiving department at the plant. His men knew they could lay off and avoid working.

"I tol Barger to get off'n his ass and get the trucks unloaded, and he turned and ran to the union boss," he had said. "The union steward chewed me out and threatened me right in front of my men," Howard complained.

"At least in a little hardware store, Howard could actually fire men who won't work," she told herself.

Her mind then wandered from the conflicts of her husband's workplace. In an undertone, she began to sing an old Scotch-Irish ballad from her childhood: "she'll be comin round the mountain when she comes....she'll be comin round the mountain when she comes...she'll be comin round the mountain...she'll be comin round the mountain...she'll be comin round the mountain when she comes."

That Spring, Henry sat in the rocker near the large window at the front of the living room. Across the road, Mr. Bone was digging out a new driveway with one of his sons. The old farmer quietly watched his neighbors work with the pick and shovel. Soon, he took his felt hat from the carriage hook near the door and walked outside. It was mid-March. Reed Finley had told Henry at the Farm Supply that Mr. Bone had been laid off from his job at Modine and was looking for work. Henry had been puzzled when Mr. Bone began coming home in a variety of new model cars.

"That boy o yorn is a real worker," he said as he crossed the road.

"He needs to lose soma his baby fat," Mr. Bone replied looking up from his pick.

"Where didja get these new cars, neighbor?" Henry queried.

"I quit the radiator factory and now I'm sellin cars," was the reply from Howard.

David began to whine as two yellow jacket wasps buzzed around his head.

"Here son," Henry said as he swatted the wasps with his hat.

"Thanks," the boy said, grinning.

"Say, Mr. Bone," Henry asked, "how much will your boss give me for my old truck?"

"Stop by Wilson Chevrolet in Paducah and you'll find out," Howard replied.

Two weeks later, Henry drove onto the parking lot at Wilson Chevrolet in the red truck. He parked it in front of the show room and walked inside.

"Howard Bone here," he asked.

"He's off today," Glen Campbell replied. "I can take care a you," he promised.

Henry looked at Glen. Glen was young and embarrassingly thin. His large nose and receding forehead gave him a comical look. Henry had heard Glen speak at the Fancy Farm political picnic the Summer before when he had run for local office.

"You jus tell Mr. Bone I came by," Henry answered.

As the farmer walked back to the red truck he muttered: "ain't buyin nuthin from that varmit," he said.

Driving off the lot of the car dealer, Henry saw Howard come out of the men's bathroom and walk onto the showroom floor.

That same week, Sam Poat loaded a 100 pound bad of hog pellets into the back of a gray truck.

"What ar you hear bout them Bone folk?" Reed Finely asked Sam.

"The whole lot wuz here yestiddy," Sam answered Reed after spitting tobacco juice onto the gravel outside the loading dock of the Farm Supply.

Reed reached into the back pocket of his overalls and pulled out an oversized leather wallet fastened to his belt by a chain. Pulling out a huge wad of bills he paid for the hog pellets.

"I think I'll stop by the Kerley farm and check on things," he drawled as he slid into the cab of his truck.

Twenty minutes later Reed's truck was in the drive of the Kerley farm. Henry and Eadie were sitting in the yard in folding aluminum chairs. They waved to Reed as he climbed out of the truck.

"Sit yourself a spell, Mr. Finley," Eadie pleaded.

"Mighty thankful for the chance, Mrs. Kerley," Reed said as he sat down next to them on an upside down galvanized steel bucket.

"I's seen Will and John Barlow goin into the unemployment office in Paduah Friday a week ago," Reed said to Henry with a knowing look on his face.

"I'm surprised you didn't go there yourself," Henry answered.

"Naw, Mr. Kerley, us farmers is doing a site better than them with the bad luck to be laid offn Modine Manufacturing," Reed said in reply.

"I'll say so, Mr. Finley," Henry answered gruffly. "The Barlows tol me that when Modine laid them off, they got nuthin but a kick in the ass," he said.

"Say, whut's goin on across the road from you here?" Reed asked.

"A whole lotta fightin by whut I can see," Henry answered.

"I hear tell from your wife, that the Bone man is a bit hard on his family," Eadie interjected, looking at Reed.

"What did Betty tell you about that? She don't tell me nuthin," Reed rasped.

"Well, Ruby Mae was buyin yarn goods at Poat's store and she tol Betty that her man works them three boys like they wuz in the Army," she related.

"I'll say he does," Henry exclaimed raising his voice and he continued, "them three boys is out in the fields till eight and nine ever night, even after their schoolin," Henry explained.

"Hell, that's good fer um," Reed interjected. "I had Marlon loading bricks onto this ol truck with Betty last night," he bragged.

"You won't seem me a havin Eadie nor any other women folk doin the same on the Kerley farm," Henry said loudly.

"You do as you please, Henry. I gotta go now folks," Reed said.

Rising from his seat on the bucket, he shook Henry's hand and made his way back to his truck.

Later that July, Eadie, Betty and Ruby Mae sat in a knitting circle in the living room of the Bone farmhouse. Ruby Mae had invited her neighbors on a Saturday when Howard and the three boys were attending a baseball game in Lone Oak. Shawna sat in her highchair next to the women. The little girl played with a plate piled high with oatmeal and raisin cookies. Suddenly, a soggy portion of cookie struck Betty in the side of the head. Betty, like Ruby Mae, was in her thirties. Unlike Eadie and Ruby Mae, who were thin, Betty was robust in figure. Around her wide waist she had tied her best flowered apron with large, ample pockets.

"She didn't mean that, did you Shawna?" Cried Betty as she picked the moist cookie out of her hair.

Ruby Mae, frowning, took her knitting needles and slapped the little girl's hands, taking care to keep the needle points away from Shawna's tender flesh. Shawna's lips began to pucker, and she began to cry.

"Here," Eadie said, walking over and sitting down with Shawna in her lap.

The girl fell silent and began to pull at the woman's neckline.

As Eadie sat playing with Shawna in her arms, the other two women continued knitting.

"Marlon has developed a liking for your David," Betty mentioned looking over at Ruby Mae.

"Them two youngins sit together ever mornin on the school bus going to Lone Oak from what David tells," Ruby Mae said.

Betty reached into an apron pocket and pulled out a large skein of yarn.

"Marlon, well he don't take a shine to jus anyone, you know," she said.

"Where'ud y'all get that fine guitar Marlon's been playin?" Ruby Mae asked her friend. "David asked for one," she said.

"Down on the river front in Paducah at Bell's Music," Betty explained, "but it'll cost your 15 dollars," she said.

Suddenly, Shawna slid down from Eadie's lap and began to run toward the kitchen from the living room where the women were sitting. Throwing down her knitting, Ruby Mae rushed to pick up the child.

"No, no, youngin, you ain't goin back there," she said as she picked Shawna up and held her to her breast.

The little girl began to kick and struggle against Ruby Mae's firm grasp.

"Bout time fer your nap, I can tell you," the slender mother muttered as she took Shawna back to her crib.

Two years went by. Henry and Becky were preparing for Christmas. It was the holiday season in Western Kentucky. It was a December evening in the living room of the Kerley house. Henry stood near the window stringing popcorn for the Christmas tree. This year, he and Mr. Bone from across the road, had walked the property of both farms looking for the right tree. They had chosen a six-foot cedar tree. The smell of cedar permeated the house.

"Becky, come on in here and lookit this," Henry said with excitement.

The 40 year-old Becky walked in from the kitchen.

"If'n only mammy was here to see it," she said looking at the string of popcorn.

Her father's mind shifted to the grave behind the house and down the hill.

"Yes, your mother alays loved this time of the year. The holidays alays give her a chance to be happy no matter what was agoin on in this world," he said.

Come over here, daddy and let's sit down," Becky said.

The father and daughter sat in the two chairs before the fire and fell silent.

After ten minutes, Becky spoke, "daddy how is your back?"

Her father reflected, "it's been gettin worse," he explained.

"What did the doctor in Paducah say when you wuz there last month?" She asked.

"He says it ain't nuthin. All them tests he done come back normal," Henry told his daughter. "But the bill don't come back nuthin, I can tell you," he said. "All that nuthin has cost me plenty," the old man explained.

Henry then felt a boring pain in the middle of his back. When the back pain first began, he had just ignored it. "As pain went, with the farmin and plowin with a mule, pain was to be expected," he had told himself. Over time, he began to get nauseated and he retched into the bathroom washing basin at night. Yes, he had been to the doctor's office in Paducah with no success. As the weeks of pain progressed, he began sleeping with a board under his mattress at night.

At nine o'clock, Becky excused herself and went to bed. After about an hour there was a knock on the door. Concerned at the time of night, Henry stood up from his chair, switched on the light on the porch and opened the door. Howard Bone stood there with a worried look on his face.

"What kin I do you for, Mr. Bone?" Henry asked as he extended his arm to shake Howard's hand.

"It's Shawna," Howard said quietly. "The little girl is a cryin and won't sleep. She passed a lotta blood outa her bottom 20 minutes ago," Howard finished.

Henry invited his neighbor inside and the two men sat down in front of the dying fire.

"I heard you had a doctor in these parts," Howard said nervously.

'I'll call Doc. Warner right now, and you jus sit here and don't worry," Henry promised putting his thin hand on Howard's shoulder.

After a few minutes on the phone, the farmer approached the car salesman.

"Tell your Ruby to get Shawna wrapped up warm. You and me is meeting Doc. Warner at the county hospital as soon as we can get there," Henry finished.

Henry and Howard stared silently as Henry's red truck bumped down the dark county road on its way to the hospital. Sitting with Shawna wrapped in blankets on his lap, Howard thought about what lay in store for him. His little girl had never been this sick before. There had been fevers and congestion of the lung, but she had recovered quickly. The only child who had really been sick was Denny with the croup. Denny had lain in bed for weeks with an oxygen tent over his head and the humidifier running. The constant, choking cough of the little boy had unnerved Ruby. She stayed in her room while Howard tended to their son. Now, with Shawna screaming, kicking and passing blood, Ruby had broken down. Leaving his wife alone with the three boys, Howard prayed she could hold together until he returned. Pulling into the graveled parking lot of the county hospital, the two men in the red truck saw a nurse standing at the door of the Emergency Room with a lantern in her hand. Once the young nurse identified Shawna in Howard's arms, she quickly took her on a gurney back to see the doctor.

Henry took up a magazine. The car salesman had trouble sitting still in the plastic and metal chair. Howard's eyes surveyed the waiting room. The faded tiles in the ceiling were cracked. In the corner, one tile hung down at an odd angle. The hum of the soda machine seemed unusually loud. Howard stood up and went over to get a bottle drink from the machine. As the bottle noisily landed in the bottom of the machine, he felt a hand on his shoulder.

"I'm Doc. Warner," he heard as he turned around.

Drawing back and looking directly into the father's eyes, Warner spoke again. "I need to put a tube up her rear and fill her bottom with fluid. That way, I can unwrap her bowels inside her. Right now, they are in a knot and it's gonna kill her if you say no," the doctor explained.

Without answering, Howard signed the papers and went back to sit down.

"You doin okay, dad?" Henry asked, looking up from his magazine.

"Don't ask me no more, neighbor," Howard replied.

"Howard, are you goin to the funeral in Lowes Sunday?" Rub Mae asked.

Her husband felt a tear start to form in his eyes.

After a moment of silence, he gathered himself together and spoke: "Reed Finley and I are goin together. Henry woulda wanted it that way," he said.

The couple fell silent as Shawna played in the floor before them. Howard reflected on the events since he and Henry had taken Shawna to the county hospital. After the girl was treated and re-leased, Henry had taken father and child home. As he walked the father to the door, the rough car salesman gave him a warm em-brace. With emotion is his voice, Howard thanked Henry for saving Shawna.

"If'n only sumpin coulda saved Henry," he now thought to himself.

In the weeks following Shawna's emergency, the farmer's back pain and vomiting had become intolerable. He started losing an alarming amount of weight and he began to weaken physically. He began sleeping on the floor with his blanket around him, no longer able to tolerate sleeping on the mattress. Another visit to Doc. Warner resulted in exploratory surgery. The results: Henry had incurable cancer and he would die soon. Doc. Warner put his hand on the old man's shoulder and expressed his sadness when he gave him the bad news.

To everyone around him, Henry was just getting old. He didn't tell anyone about his diagnosis, even his daughter. But Becky knew better than anyone, that her father was dying. It was just a matter of time until one morning Henry did not get up to feed the mule and collect the eggs as was his habit. Becky found the body stiff and cold on the floor by the bed, with the blanket clutched in his dead hands.

It was a cold February, Sunday morning when Howard Bone awoke to go to the funeral in Lowes, Kentucky. He left Ruby and the children asleep and dressed in his best blue suit. On most Sunday mornings, Ruby would tie his necktie. This morning he tied it himself. The frozen brown grass crumpled beneath his shoes as he walked to his truck. The sky was a mournful gray color. The heater in the truck had not worked in some time, so Reed Finley and Howard Bone sat hunched in their seats during the 30 mile drive to the Lowe's Funeral Home. Walking into the visitation room, the two men sat on the back row.

"I don't care whut they say. Henry don't look no good to me in this coffin," Reed had said in an undertone as the two men stood looking at their friend.

The body didn't look like Henry at all, as they discussed later.

"He was alays thin, but there is nuthin left t'day but bones," Howard had mentioned.

After the viewing and a brief word from the two men to Becky, there was a short homily by the Presbyterian minister. Friends and neighbors drove in silence to the grave site. After the grave-side service Howard began to feel better. Henry was in a better place than this world. Howard was sure of that. Taking a Bible from his back pocket, he picked up a white carnation from one of the bouquets and pressed the flower between its pages.

Jeremy opened the Herald Leader and searched for the racing
news of the day. The Fall Session had begun and the who's who
of Fayette County would meet at the thoroughbred races. Parking
was always difficult across from Bluegrass Field, the airport near
Keeneland. On this Sunday, driving out Versailles Pike, Jeremy
was able to find a small spot near the entrance to Keeneland for
his Volkswagen Beetle. Gnarled, tall oaks lined the entrance to the
clubhouse. Most of the spectators were already in the grandstands,
mixed drinks in hand. The entire spectacle of thoroughbred racing
in Kentucky began in the nineteenth century, but by the 1940's the
racing industry had become charged with oil money from Texas.
Texans owned the many stately horse farms-they were not owned
by the Kentucky tobacco farmers and whiskey brewers. Sixty
years later, in the early twenty-first century, the Texans sold out to
the royalty of the Middle East. It was odd, Jeremy thought, that
men from foreign countries owned the horses and the land, because you would not find them walking around Lexington, and they
were not at the track today.

In the courtyard behind the grandstand, one of the horses was up
for review. It was a handsome beast, a chestnut thoroughbred with
white forelocks. The animal was tall, about 16 hands high, and
had a nervous temperament of a great racer. Interested spectators
peered at the horse in admiration. Jeremy stood away from the
hindquarters. He was well aware that one, well-place kick could
create serious injury. A stable hand carefully walked the animal
around the graveled ring. Jeremy noticed a dark-haired young
woman with an hourglass figure in the background. She had strik-
ing looks and a quiet demeanor. A bit on the short side, she was
probably just over five feet tall. She looked foreign. Interested, he
walked over.

"Nice animal, isn't he?" He said, glancing at the young woman.

"Yes, he is a beauty," she answered.

"Are you a horse lover" she then asked as she looked up into Jeremy's face.

Jeremy was startled by the challenge in her eyes. He began to cough but regained his composure and tried to stifle the subtle shake in his voice.

"I am not an expert, but I have had an interest in horses since a young age. As a boy in Western Kentucky, I was somewhat obsessed with books of great racehorses of the past. You might be familiar with them; horses like Citation, Whirlaway and Affirmed,'" he said.

"Yes," the woman gushed, warming to his presence. "I am from a family with many years of horse breeding behind them," she said.

Jeremy's interest was piqued, and he pressed the young woman for details.

She began rather mysteriously, "my father's family has been breeding thoroughbreds for more than a century. In the early years, the breeding stock was brought from England," she said.

Jeremy was aware that the thoroughbred was an English breed and had been brought to America from England. It had originated from both British and Arab blood lines. He listened for any foreign accent in the speaker, but was unable to detect one.

"The thoroughbred is the ultimate racehorse," he broke in. "In my part of the state of Kentucky, the horse to own was the Saddle-bred. As you may know, the Saddle-bred originated in this area around Lexington," he said.

"No, but this is fascinating," she replied. "By the way, I'm Shakira," she said and the young woman extended her hand.

As Jeremy shook her small hand, he noticed that she had a rather soft grasp.

"I'm Jeremy," he replied.

"And what do you do, Mr. Jeremy?" Shakira asked as she looked questioningly up at him.

"I'm a medical resident at the Chandler Medical Center," he said.

"You don't say, Mr. Jeremy," and Shakira broke into a smile.

"I'll tell you what, come to this address next Saturday at noon, and I'll show you our stables," she suggested.

After the medical team had completed their rounds the next Saturday, Jeremy finished his notes in the charts and pulled out a scrap of paper. An address on Tate's Creek Road was listed. He knew the area well. There were a number of elegant horse farms there. Driving out of town, he passed New Circle Road and then proceeded into Fayette County on Tate's Creek Road. A large gray mailbox was at the front entrance to a small farm at the address. He made a quick right turn into the driveway and proceeded to the main house. White framed fences lined the fields surrounded by numerous sycamore trees. Jeremy and his Volkswagen Bug pulled up to a large house with wooden siding.

An older man was standing on the porch and introduced himself as Jeremy approached him. "I'm Mr. Reza, Shakira's father, young man. How do you do?" He inquired.

The gentleman had graying hair with a short beard and mustache. Jeremy held out his hand, but Mr. Reza waved him over to the stables.

"The woman you seek, my daughter, is waiting for you," he said.

Within the stables, Shakira stood to the side of a bay mare. She was washing the animal with a large, warm soaked sponge.

"This is Maud. She will foal soon, Mr. Jeremy," she said.

The mare's stomach was swollen with pregnancy, and she had a healthy sheen to her coat. Shakira walked around to the front of the horse and stroked her soft nose.

"Where did you get her?" Jeremy asked.

"She was a gift from my grandfather in Doha City," Shakira continued, "and she has excellent blood lines."

"I can see that," the medical resident replied and then he said, "she is quite impressive."

"But what about you, young doctor? Where are you from? Please, sit over here," the woman said.

The two young people then sat on a sturdy bench to the side of the center aisle of the stables.

Jeremy began his story. "I am from the western part of the state of Kentucky, near the confluence of the Ohio and Mississippi Rivers. The land and the people are more like Mississippi than Kentucky. The weather is hot, and the land is flat. Agriculture is king. Cash crops are harvested with a combine. The most important news in my hometown is the hog market and soybean report. All of my uncles are farmers," he said.

"But you are a doctor. How have you afforded such expensive schooling?" She asked.

Jeremy smiled, "it's the magic of scholarships. In many ways, I am the product of the educational welfare system," he continued.

"Dear doctor, do you ride?" Shakira asked.

"Not really," Jeremy replied. "As a young boy, I dreamed of owning my own horse. My father and I went to horse auctions, but in the end, we just couldn't afford the animal nor the land," he said.

"Well," the young woman replied, "you are always welcome on our farm, and you may visit at any time."

Jeremy felt a sudden rush of pleasure, and his face told Shakira what he felt.

Shakira then told her story. "My father was born in Doha City and he was given this farm as a young man. He has dedicated his life to the breeding of fine horses. Mother joined him from Qatar, and I was born here in Lexington. You see, young Jeremy, I do not require one of your famous "green cards." My grandparents have never been to the United States, but as I have said, they gave me the lovely Maud you have seen. She is so beautiful, young doctor, isn't she? My only brother, Shareef, was educated in London, but now resides here in Kentucky, in the same city as you and I," she said.

During the soliloquy, Jeremy studied the face of the speaker intently. She had an olive complexion, dark shoulder length hair and brown eyes. Her nose and facial features were finely chiseled and feminine. There was something of the fierceness of the Arabian sun in her manner, but she was ultimately charming. "Come with me," she insisted, and they proceeded toward the house.

Once inside the front door, Shakira walked to her father's study and Jeremy followed her. Within the room, the patriarch was working at his desk.

As they entered, he looked up. "Take a seat daughter," he instructed.

The two young people sat down on the couch and Mr. Reza spoke, "tell me about yourself, young man."

Jeremy began. "I met Shakira at the races and she asked me to your stables. I am in the Internal Medicine Residency at the Chandler Medical Center. I have lived here in Lexington for ten years, this Fall. I have been a life-long admirer of thoroughbred race horses and horse racing," he said.

Mr. Reza then interjected: "we are rebuilding our stables currently. Our finest stud died three months ago, but our best mare, Maud, will foal soon."

"Papa, how are the negotiations for the new stud coming along?" Shakira asked.

The father continued: "the negotiations have broken down, but I plan to hire outstanding studs for our mares. If the subsequent yearlings do well at the races, I will save the best of them for our permanent stud," he explained.

Mr. Reza then stood up and brought a book over and placed it on Jeremy's lap.

"Recognize this horse?" He asked.

The winner's circle of a prominent handicap race at Churchill Downs from previous years was displayed.

"I can say that I do, sir, that is Stamina and his jockey, Joey Brown," Jeremy said.

"Good," Shakira's father said. "My daughter had found one of our own, although I would guess that you are a Christian lover of horses," he said.

"Yes, everyone in my town was Protestant, Christian, you are correct," Jeremy answered.

"Never mind, young man," was the reply.

After a lengthy discussion on racehorses, the time for Jeremy to leave was approaching. The visit had gone well. In Shakira, he had found a fellow horse lover. The two young people had much in common, although their backgrounds could not have been more disparate. Shakira walked the resident doctor to his car and as they approached the car, she stopped.

"Jeremy, before you go, isn't there something you have forgotten to ask me?" She asked.

There was entreaty in her brown eyes. The young man felt a chill. No sudden recollection of what he had forgotten came to his mind. He struggled to say something appropriate. There was an embarrassing silence.

She then said: "I will be at the Saturday meets for the rest of the season," and just as suddenly, she turned and walked back to her father's house.

Jeremy climbed behind the wheel of his car, and he made sure to save the note with Shakira's address.

Two weeks passed before Jeremy had a chance to visit Keeneland. The prior weekend he had been waylaid by patients at the hospital. There had been several admissions to the Cardiac Intensive Care Unit, and the patients had not done well. There had been complications: complex arrhythmias and patients with congestive heart failure. A few patients had died suddenly. Investigations into the quality of care the residents had provided ensued. As a junior resident, Jeremy had been responsible to the Chief Resident. All the busywork had been performed by the grunts: the third-year medical students. Finally, he pulled the Volkswagen into the parking lot at the races.

The usual crowd was there. This Saturday was crowded. The young man surveyed the area for the Muslim woman with dark hair. The faces of the women seemed to blur in his mind, and his memories of Shakira seemed vague. The situation was his own fault. He had failed to get her phone number or make a date to revisit the horse farm. He had made this mistake with other women, never to see them again.

At the close of the racing day, Jeremy felt defeated. People were filing out of the grandstands and heading to the grassy parking area. Walking to the end of the drive and approaching the Volkswagen, he thought he felt a slight tug on his sleeve and he turned slightly in the direction of the sensation. At once, he felt two arms tightly wound around his torso and a light body pressed against him.

"Young doctor, I knew you would come," she murmured.

Shakira was there at his side, like a flash of incredibly good luck. Relief and happiness flooded his mind. Jeremy then held her slightly back so he could see her face, and he held her with both of her arms in his grasp.

"I have to know how to find you Shakira. I can't leave finding you to chance again; it is too great a risk," he told her.

She smiled a bright smile and they sat down together in his car. Two two young people shared their feelings, talked at length about their worries and hopes, and exchanged contact information.

The future of the Reza farm depended upon the birth of foals. Stamina, the primary stud of the farm had passed away. Shakira's father had erected a monument to the stallion in front of the exercise ring. Stamina was well-known among the owners of the horse farms in the area. Early one morning, Shakira dressed in her work clothes and made her way to the stables. The stable hands had already given the mares and colts, including Maud, their morning water followed by oats. To give a horse oats before water is to risk life-threatening colic. After the oat bags were empty, the horses were walked. Maud was taken out and exercised. Physical exertion is important for a pregnant mare. Shakira then rubbed her down and brushed her. Taking her by the halter, Shakira led her back into her stall, which was filled with fresh straw.

After her morning routine, Shakira returned to the main house. She entered the kitchen and sat down at the table. Her thoughts wandered back to Saturday at Keeneland. For two weeks, she had wondered if she would see Jeremy again. In Shakira's life, the young men had come and gone at random. Being from a foreign family, there had been troubles with her relationships with American men. These men didn't appreciate her family's origins in the Middle East. The truth was that there was distrust of her family, especially her father. As Shakira engaged in this reverie, she didn't notice that Abdul had entered the room and sat down opposite her at the table.

"Daughter," he stated, and Shakira was shaken from her thoughts, "who is this Christian man to you?" He asked.

The young woman shuddered. She had been through this before with her father.

"Father, he is a kind young man, but very shy," she answered.

"What can a Christian man be to a Muslim girl?' He asked her.

Shakira's voice trembled as she said: "but we are not living in the Middle East, my father, and there aren't many of our kind here in Lexington."

The older man was touched by this. He genuinely loved his daughter. He approached her, touching her cheek with his hand.

He continued, "just be careful. You know what his people have done to our kind," he said.

Although Shakira had been born and educated in America, her father had taught her the history of her race. Europeans had invaded their lands and cruelly slaughtered Muslim women and men for centuries. After World War One, the British had occupied Qatar and treated its people like slaves and dogs. In Qatar, Europeans had a bad reputation among the local people.

Shakira sat alone in her bedroom with her thoughts. There was something in the manner of this doctor that attracted her. She found her thoughts constantly centering on him. At night, she dreamed of being his wife, although she had a very poor under-standing of what this would mean. Her mother had died when she was young, soon after she had been born. As a girl, Shakira had been raised by her father, who had never remarried and who was in perpetual mourning for the loss of his wife. Abdul had tried dating, but Western women could not tolerate his manner. He was over-bearing and dogmatic.

Shareef Reza, M.D. walked into the fifth-floor chart room of the Chandler Medical Center. This was the beginning of his fourth year of post-graduate medical education. He had the honor of being selected as Chief Resident of the Department of Internal Medicine. The position came with significant responsibility as well as recog-nition. Under his guidance, there were fifteen resident physicians: five interns, five junior residents, and five senior residents. The program was competitive, although it was not in the top ten around the country. Still, the University of Kentucky had a regional pres-ence, and the Chandler Medical Center was the most prestigious hospital in the Bluegrass State. The third-year medical students were writing their patient notes for the day. To them, Shareef was an important man.

He surveyed the group: they were above average. The previous quarter there had been problems: tardiness, incomplete entries into the charts, and there had been one expulsion from the medical school. A transfer student from SUNY Downstate in Brooklyn had refused to follow his intern's orders and had gone rogue treating pa-tients on his own. After proven documentation of this student's in-subordination, he had been permanently expelled from school. The Dean of the College of Medicine regretted doing this. The student from Brooklyn had made honors in his pre-clinical years.

Jeremy had learned his lesson after his first visit to the Reza farm and finding Shakira, by chance, at Keeneland two weeks later. He now had her telephone number and her address written down. That was no guarantee of success with her, however, as he well knew. A young professional in his late twenties he had plenty of failures with women. As a serious student with a meager income, there had not been time for a social life in past years. Now spending most of his time in the hospital, most of the women he met were divorced, single mothers employed by the hospital. They all had their eyes on the young doctors as potential mates. Still, even if he were married, there would be conflict and discord. The resident physician salary was low. As an intern, Jeremy had started at $25,000 per year. This meant that low-end housing was all that he could afford.

Jeremy and Shakira sat having lunch in the hospital cafeteria. The young woman's eyes were fixed on her boyfriend. He was on the thin side with light brown hair, and he was of medium height. His looks were pleasing to her. He was not too good-looking.

 "If he were a lady-killer," she reflected, "it would be challenging to keep him from other women."

He was a serious young man, "but how serious," she wondered, "is he about me?"

She reached across the table and straightened his crumpled neck tie.

"Father would like to have you to lunch at the farm this Sunday, Jeremy." She said.

She brushed her long black hair back behind her ears.

"Maud's colt is being weaned and the vet has given us high hopes that he will be a strong yearling," she continued.

Jeremy looked up to see a twinkle in Shakira's eyes. She turned her head and looked out the window.

"I will definitely be there," he answered, "what time do the festivities begin?" He asked.

She answered, "I am going to be anxious and very upset with you if you are any later than one p.m. Sunday."

The medical resident looked straight into her face, "I wouldn't have that happen, ever," he said. "But what if the old Bug has trouble making it onto Tates Creek Pike?" He asked.

"I have a new BMW and triple A, young doctor so don't worry," she finished.

Shakira stirred a large pot of lamb stew in the kitchen of the farm on Tates Creek Pike. The lambs had been humanely slaughtered, as was the custom in the Middle East. They had been raised locally and brought in from the stockyards in a flatbed truck with high wooden railings. The worn rubber tires of the truck had bumped uncomfortably along the narrow roads of Fayette County. After butchering, the scraps that were left were placed in metal pails for the farm's two collie dogs. Steam from the sauce of the stew gave a pleasant smell of tomatoes and celery throughout the room. She had made unleavened pita bread and placed a plate of the bread on the table. Bowls of pureed chickpeas mixed with olive oil were prepared as well. Mr. Reza met Jeremy at the door and the two men made their way to the kitchen.

"Young daughter, you have done an excellent job this afternoon," Mr. Reza remarked.

Shakira looked up. Jeremy noticed that her hair had been bobby-pinned back. She was dressed in jodhpurs and a riding shirt. Earlier that morning she had exercised the yearlings, and her brown leather riding switch stood in the corner of the kitchen between the stove and the plaster wall.

The young Arab woman placed glasses, plates and bowls on the heavy wooden table. The two men sat down with Shakira to eat. Mr. Reza was quiet for the first several minutes. Jeremy and Shakira sat opposite one another.

"Father," Shakira said, "how are things going with the six yearlings?" She asked.

"They seem to be talented," her father replied. "I am putting up three at the yearling sales this Spring," he related

"That should help the bottom line, Mr. Reza," Jeremy mentioned.

"Yes, and with the proceeds from the sale, I think I can afford that talented mare from Abemarle Farm," Abdul said.

"Which one is that father?" Shakira asked.

He answered: "she is the offspring of the Derby winner, Stalwart," he answered.

"Stalwart! He has been an excellent stud and has already fathered two winners of the Preakness," Shakira exclaimed. "I must say, I am impressed, father, and I am excited about the addition of this mare to our stables. Maud has some age on her. She is almost 20 years old, and our other mares are over ten years old," she replied.

"If Maud has any fillies, you can keep one for breeding," Jeremy suggested.

"That is the plan, but how are things at the Medical Center?" Mr. Reza asked.

Before Jeremy could start on a speech about the Medical Center, Shareef Reza, Shakira's brother, walked in and sat down to eat.

"I can answer that," Shareef said. "The Internal Medicine Residency has just passed another accreditation by the American Board of Internal Medicine."

"Isn't that a relief, my brother," Shakira said.

"Yes, sister, especially since as Chief Resident this is a new experience for me," Shareef said.

"I still have to pass my Internal Medicine Boards in a year and a half, so things for me are in limbo," Jeremy mentioned.

"The University program has always had a healthy pass record, so I think that will be a given," Shareef answered Jeremy.

"I hope you are right, Dr. Reza," Jeremy muttered as he looked down at his lamb stew.

"My darling, you will have no problem," Shakira said as she reached over and put her hand on his shoulder.

The young doctor's gloom lifted.

After having lunch, Jeremy and Shakira walked around the grounds of the horse farm. The mares and the foals grazed in the front field. The yearlings were kept behind the house in a large pasture by the stables. Shakira let her mind wander and she reflected on the situation of the Reza family.

"Jeremy, my father is getting older and he is not in good health. Shareef is the only hope that the farm will continue on in our name. I have cousins in Doha, but we really aren't close. Frankly," the woman confided, "my relatives back in Qatar don't approve of a Muslim woman choosing her own fate and living in America," she said.

Jeremy stood silent and then spoke: "Shareef must be careful, Shakira. The Dean of the Medical School does not like foreign medical graduates and there have been difficulties with the faculty since Shareef was chosen as Chief Medical Resident," he said.

"Yes," she answered. "My brother has mentioned this to me, but we three are here in America, and we aren't going back to Qatar. My mother, after all, chose to be buried here."

Walking to the front of the farm together, Jeremy knew there was more in Shakira's future than she could realize. The Muslim girl was his only serious relationship since high school, and he was not looking further. She seemed right for a Kentucky boy from the Jackson Purchase. As they parted, he felt thankful that he seemed to be getting along with her brother at the University Hospital. It was well known that despite the Dean's prejudice, Shareef was in line for a Cardiology Fellowship after his Chief Resident year, that is , if the Chief of Cardiology had any say in the matter.

The year had gone well for Jeremy. He continued to see Shakira and their relationship deepened. Things at the Medical Center were turbulent. As junior residents, the Internal Medicine Boards were constantly on the minds of Jeremy and his contemporaries. After four years of college, four years of medical school, and then residency, if they failed the Boards, their career was over before it had started. Some of the less dedicated residents began cutting rounds to study. Those who remained on the wards taking care of patients picked up the slack. Shareef had counseled the less than honorable residents, but to no avail. Finally, it had come to the point that someone had to be cut from the program to make a point. Shareef went over the list of those who consistently cut rounds. After choosing his victim, he called the secretary of the Department of Internal Medicine to schedule an appointment with Dr. Bush, the Chairman of Internal Medicine.

Shareef sat in the waiting room of Dr. Bush's office. He had already notified Dr. Green, the resident, that a meeting with him and Dr. Bush was scheduled for 10 a.m. When called back to Dr. Bush's office, Shareef noticed that Dr. Green and Dr. Bush were already present. As the meeting began, Shareef recounted the resident's many infractions. Things, however, were not going as he had planned. Dr. Bush seemed stubborn and unsympathetic to Shareef's concerns.

After a few minutes, the Chairman said in a loud voice to his chief resident: "now just a minute mister. My secretary, Sandy, has double checked these numbers and they just don't add up. And if you really want to get personal," Bush then stood up and got red in the face, "it has come to my attention that you were absent from Cardiology Clinic last Thursday, and there was no one to take your place."

Shareef sat dumbfounded. He had asked one of the junior residents to cover for him for the day he was absent from the Cardiology Clinic.

Bush continued: "And if you want to know the rest of the story, the day your were absent, a patient with an echo cardiogram confirming cardiac tamponade and congestive heart failure was sent home from the clinic without followup and died," Bush said angrily.

Shareef apologized and made for the door. Things were serious. As he sat in the resident off-duty room, one of the interns ambled by and told him there was a letter for him in his cubicle. Anxious, he hurried over, picked up the letter and read through it. It was a letter of suspension from the program signed by Dr. Bush and co-signed by the Dean.

Jeremy was not surprised when he heard about Shareef's suspension. Rumors of Islamophobic thinking among the faculty were widespread.

After an unusually grim murder at a military recruiting center in Chattanooga, the Dean had been overheard saying to Dr. Bush: "I don't want any more Muslim doctors in my hospital."

Since Shareef's suspension, Shakira had not called Jeremy. The Reza family had maintained a strict silence. Jeremy rang her number without getting an answer. Worried, he climbed into the Beetle and drove to the farm. He waited on the front porch. After knocking on the door, he entered and walked from the front hall to Abdul's study. He called out for Shakira. He heard a faint answer from inside the study and found her sitting on the couch crying.

When Shakira saw Jeremy, she bent over and hid her face in her lap. The young internist sat down at her side and took her face in his hands. He kissed the young woman, and then tenderly brushed her tears away from her eyes.

"I have a plan, dearest, call Shareef and Abdul into the study to meet me," he told her.

Shakira composed herself and then rose slowly and left the room. Within minutes, she had returned with her brother and father. The four of them sat down together.

Jeremy began to speak: "It is well known around Lexington that the owners of Calumet Farm gave the Dean of the Medical School the money he needed to build the new cancer center. Do you know these people, Abdul?" He asked.

"Of course I know them," the elder Reza replied. Abdul then said out loud, "my relatives in Qatar have extensive ties with the south- ern kingdom."

"Do you think the Saudis would meet with you, me and Shareef if we invited them over the Tates Creek?" Jeremy asked.

"I have every reason to believe that they will, young man," Abdul said with animation, and then he continued, "I will have them over within the week."

Several weeks went by. Dr. Bush sat at his desk early in the morn- ing. At eight a.m. when his secretary, Sandy, was at her desk he asked her to come into his office.

"Have you typed the letter to Shareef Reza that I dictated yester- day?" He queried. Sandy became nervous.

The news had been all over the hospital about Shareef's suspension a few weeks before.

"Uh, yes, you mean the letter about his termination from the University?" She asked.

"That's the one, well, throw the damn thing away. Oh, and call Shareef and ask for a one-on-one meeting with me, in this office tomorrow at noon," he said.

Sandy retreated to her desk and within one hour the news was circulating around the department about the meeting between Shareef and Bush.

It was noon in Dr. Bush's office the next day. Shareef sat meekly in a chair waiting for the chairman to arrive. As was his custom, Dr. Bush always made the chief residents wait. Bush stalked into his office and quickly sat down.

"You are pretty lucky, young man," he began. "The Dean has intervened in my business here in this department and demanded that your suspension be lifted, and that you be reinstated as Chief Resident. Frankly, I don't mind telling you that I was firmly against this, but what does my opinion matter in this hospital? Not a whole lot, I can tell you," he related in a tense voice.

"Yes, sir," Shareef answered.

Privately, Shareef knew the inside story behind his reinstatement. The Saudis had threatened to withdraw all financial support from the University Hospital and had threatened to enlist other Muslims in Lexington to follow suit if Shareef was not reinstated. As owners of all the horse farms in the Bluegrass Region of Kentucky, the Middle Eastern oil millionaires were clearly the wealthiest and most influential backers of the entire University of Kentucky not just the university hospital.

"That's it, you are dismissed," Dr. Bush concluded.

Outside of Dr. Bush's office, Jeremy and Shakira were waiting. As the Chief Resident left Bush's office, he had a quick huddle with his sister and her boyfriend. The good news came as no surprise to them, but they were still relieved at the outcome.

Jeremy and Shakira sat silently on the couch in Abdul's study. The young doctor had one arm around her, and she leaned on him with her head resting on his shoulder. Her thoughts centered on the future and what might be in store for her. Jeremy was soon to take his Internal Medicine Boards and he seemed very devoted to her. Her brother was finishing up the year as Chief Resident and had been accepted into the Cardiology Fellowship with steady encouragement by the Chairman of Cardiology.

With his free hand, Jeremy was thumbing through one of Abdul's books on the history of thoroughbred racing in the Bluegrass.

Putting down the book, Jeremy turned toward his girlfriend and said: "I think this new colt of Maud's is going to be a talented racer."

"Of that, Jeremy, I am very sure," Shakira answered.

Jimmy

Jimmy's heels made a clacking sound as he walked down the street. The hard surface of the concrete scraped against the shiny heels of his new shoes. It was a cold morning in Harlan, Kentucky.

"I guess it must be down to 22 degrees this morning," Jimmy said to himself.

The nearby river had a cold look, and fog rose from its surface this morning. It had rained the night before and the water in the river was high and rough. It was not known how many people had drowned in the river over the years. The number was considerable. Five years before, the body of a young blonde woman, who had waitressed at the cafe next to the hardware store where Jimmy worked, had been found hung under bushes on the river's bend just past downtown. The waitress had been a friend of Jimmy's older sister, Linda.

The bell on the door of the hardware store where Jimmy worked rang as he entered.

"You're right on time, youngster," Mr. Hardaway, the owner, remarked as Jimmy tied a faded apron around his waist.

After a two-year stint in the Navy in Virginia Beach, the young man had returned to his hometown. When he left Harlan for the east coast of Virginia, his plan was never to return. Things had changed. While arranging shovels and rakes in the corner, Jimmy's mind reverted to earlier years.

Jimmy's father was a widower. He had raised his two children alone. Income for this small family was provided by the local deep-shaft coal mines. Stuart, the father, had lived most of his life below the surface of Harlan. There he found back-breaking work. As a boy, Jimmy had been groomed for a life in the mines. The pay in the mines was superior to many jobs, even the jobs of college-educated folk in the town. As a coal miner, the boy would not have to leave home. The main shaft of the coal mine was an easy walk down Jackson Street, not far from where Stuart, Jimmy, and Linda lived. For years, Jimmy had taken his father lunch at noon. There he met the other miners. As time went on, Jimmy's father had developed a nagging cough and he often coughed up black phlegm in the evenings. Stuart would rise periodically from the supper table to spit the thick black substance into the kitchen sink.

"Daddy, you need more greens and red-skinned potatoes," Linda would say.

"Try working out at the Y dad," Jimmy would suggest.

"I reckon what I really need is more of these fried apple pies," the father would reply.

Working at the hardware store, time passed quickly. In the early morning there was an eight a.m. rush. This was the time the local building contractors entered the store. Mr. Hardaway, the store owner, had developed a large retail business. His store was closer to the construction sites than the large, wholesale hardware outlets. This meant that if a building contractor ran out of supplies it was easier to run by Hardaway's than drive all the way to the big box stores outside the limits of Harlan. Since he was the son of a coal miner, when Jimmy first took the job, he didn't know hardware. His boss had taken the effort to train Jimmy. Mr. Hardaway taught Jimmy everything that 40 years in the hardware business had taught him.

"Mornin, Mrs. Peeler,' Jimmy drawled at noon as the middle-aged widow and her shapely daughter entered the store.

"I need some cleanin fluid, Jimmy," the woman replied.

"Yes, ma'am if you'll step right over here," Jimmy said.

The three: Mrs. Peeler, her daughter Kathy, and the eager clerk walked over to the west end of the store. As Jimmy discussed the pros and cons of the different cleaners, Mrs. Peeler made her choice. Kathy stood silently by. Silence was one of Kathy's chief attributes, besides her jet black hair and her clear, white complexion. Jimmy had been eager to make the girl's acquaintance. However, she had never spoken in his presence, and she always came with her mother. Whenever the young girl entered the hardware store, she walked with a bouncy gait and cheerily swung her head from side to side.

"Well, daddy, sit yourself right down in this easy chair," Linda quipped.

Stuart propped his feet up on a round stool and leaned back in his seat. Linda took off his leather shoes and thick woolen socks. Her father looked up at the ceiling. The daughter then proceeded to give her father his nightly foot massage. In the next room, Jimmy had come home late from Hardaway's and had made his way back to the kitchen. After eating a bowl of pole beans and a piece of corn bread, he began washing the nightly dishes. As the clean dishes began to dry in the wire rack on the counter, Jimmy hung up his washing rag and joined his father and sister in the living room.

After the foot massage, Linda sat across the room in a large bean bag chair.

"The boss said today that we are behind on our monthly quota of coal," the old man explained.

"Why don't he join in then?" Jimmy asked.

"I guess he is too busy countin all his money in the bank," Stuart replied.

'You know the United Mine Workers have tried to move into Harlan," Jimmy related.

"Don't I know it Jimmy, and them's that joined em are full of buck shot," he replied.

"My friends say their kind are only makin trouble, daddy. Don't you hang with their kind," the daughter pleaded.

"Don't worry, Linny. I've always been a card-carrying member of the Grand Ol Party, and I ain't a changin now," the old man bragged.

Stuart ran the coal cutting machine that tore the black bituminous coal from the seams deep beneath the surface of Eastern Kentucky. Being the man closest to the coal seam, Stuart was exposed to the majority of the coal dust. The dust was largely invisible as he worked, but it had to be kept down. Large machines sprayed water to settle the dust and the mines were vented. Coal dust caused "Black Lung." Stuart had heard the name "Black Lung," from the pulmonologist that he saw at the University of Kentucky Hospital in Lexington.

"Your lungs are 20 plus years older than you are, Mr. Duncan," the pulmonologist had said to him.

"Don't matter none to me Doc. Minin is all I've ever known, and it's all my daddy and granddaddy knew," Stuart replied.

"That so," the doctor had said. "Well, I guess all your people knew what they were getting into then," he concluded.

Driving east on the Mountain Parkway from Lexington to Harlan, Stuart left the rolling fields of the Bluegrass for the hard scrabble hills of the Appalachian Mountains. A few miles from Harlan, he pulled his truck off the Mountain Parkway onto a secondary road. It was easy to get lost on the narrow, winding blacktop that led from the Mountain Parkway to Harlan.

 The roads ran along the stony mountain streams and small rivers of the Appalachians. This was the only land that was passable in the mountains. The remainder of the land was steep, and covered with a tangle of impenetrable rhododendron, confer and hardwood forest. Other than coal, the only other way to make a living here was lumber.

A combination of deep shaft mining and deforestation from lumber harvest had practically denuded Eastern Kentucky in the late nineteenth century. Since then, as the lumber industry moved to the great northwest of America and from there north to Canada, the trees of the eastern mountains had made a comeback. "Prettiest country I ever saw," Stuart thought as his truck wound its way toward his home.

"Wouldn't live anywhere else," he thought to himself.

"Daddy, what did the professor say about your lungs today?" Asked Linda that night in the living room.

"I have the lungs of an 80 year-old and they won't last much longer," Stuart replied.

"I have seen you struggle to breath," Jimmy said. "There's more coal dust in your chest than on the bricks of our chimney," the son concluded.

"The boss is on to me," his father replied. "You know, these days I'm havin trouble just walkin each morning to the mine shaft," the father related.

"Jus quit daddy, you don't need no Cadillac no way," Linda advised.

"I might not have much choice," Linny, he replied. "Last week the foreman put me on probation for gettin back from lunch late," he said.

Jimmy had been watching his father closely the past few months. Stuart was getting noticeably thinner. The bones of his chest protruded through wiry, gray hair. His legs were thin with prominent square knees. His back had become stooped with a prominent curvature that worsened when Stuart stood and walked.

"My dad is an old man," the son realized.

Linda was Stuart's favorite child, not that he didn't had love for his son. Since an early age, she had been a substitute helpmate for the widower. She was attractive, although a bit on the plump side, and she took the household chores seriously. She washed the clothes, cooked most of the food, and found time to give the lino-leum floors a healthy scrubbing each week. Her boyfriend, Marlon, whom she had dated since age fifteen, was like another son to Stuart. Marlon lived a few blocks away in a rented room and was a fellow miner.

"Can I run to the grocery Linny?" Marlon asked Friday evening as he entered the front door.

"I need brown eggs, lard and flour, Marlon, you're such a dear," she replied. "Daddy, shake the dust off those overalls and get yourself into the tub for a good scrubbin," Linda ordered.

"Yes, ma'am, yes," her father replied, as he walked across the bed-room in long johns.

"The city water is hot tonight. I drawed it already and it's steamin," Linda said.

After Stuart finished scrubbing himself, he put on fresh clothes. By that time Marlon had returned from the grocer.

After dinner, Stuart and Marlon talked Harlan news as Linda sat in the rocker knitting.

"I have talked to Jimmy till I am red in the face, Mr. Duncan," Marlon said. "That boy of yours has sumpin agin the good money of the mines," he concluded.

"It's the dark he don't like, Marlon. It's not the hard work; he ain't no sissy no way," the older man said.

"I think it is that Kathy Peeler and her mom comin into Hardaway's every Satiday mornin, Mr. Duncan," Marlon related.

"Now that girl and her mom can work," Stuart mentioned. "They do all the cleanin for half the folks' homes on this side of Harlan, I'll have you know," he said. "When I go on Social Security and quit workin down the hole, I'm havin them help Linny," Stuart mentioned.

"Jimmy, he's never gonna quit pinin for that Kathy,though," Marlon continued.

"Won't do no good, Marlon. She's been seein that Puckett boy goin on two years now," Stuart said.

On the weekends, after Hardaway's closed, Jimmy headed for the local high school basketball game. He didn't see many friends there, however. Most of his friends from high school were either married and had young families, or they had moved away. None-theless, the games were upbeat for Jimmy since the cheerleaders were pretty. Harlan High Senior Varsity had a long losing streak. The losing streak had been going on as long as Jimmy could re-member. It just seemed to him, that the sons of the Harlan min-ers couldn't hit a basket compared to the young men of Pikeville. During the basketball season, it was cold outside the gym, but the bodies of the Harlan young people kept the inside warm. The oil burning furnaces of the old gymnasium helped as well.

Eddie Puckett and Kathy Peeler invariably made it to the games, and that was a plus as far as Jimmy was concerned. Kathy was several years Jimmy's junior. By the time he had gotten out of the Navy, she was just entering high school. Despite her good looks, Kathy was not popular in her class. For one thing, she never said a word. Very few of her classmates knew anything of her life outside of school.During the week, Marlon stopped by the hardware store.

"Why don't you get outa this store and do something, Jimmy?" Marlon complained one afternoon. "Linda and I are going to the movie pictures on Saturday night, and you're invited," he told Jimmy.

"I don't know Marlon. My old car needs a new alternator," Jimmy mentioned.

"You just put a rebuilt engine into that old jalopy. How much more are you going to spend on it?" Marlon asked.

"I gotta have wheels, Marlon. What do you expect from me? Hardaway's don't pay that much," Jimmy related.

"Ask the old man for a raise then," Marlon advised.

"Hardaway is as broke as you and me, Marlon," Jimmy conveyed.

Rather than going to the pictures with Linda and Marlon, Jimmy had taken up going to Saturday night revivals at the local Pentecostal church. Mrs. Peeler always attended and, occasionally, Kathy was there. And Kathy didn't seem to be bringing Eddie with her to church. Eddie was Catholic and this was a sore point between Kathy and Eddie. Around town, it was well known that the Pentecostals and the Catholics didn't have much to do with each other.

Pastor Mark had been preaching about 30 minutes on this particular night.

"He don't seem to have much point to his sermon tonight," thought Jimmy as he sat in the middle of the Pentecostal sanctuary.

The hardware clerk spent most of the evening inspecting the large lamps that hung from the ceiling of the sanctuary by heavy metal chains.

"I am afraid to think what might happen should one of these chains ever break," he thought. "Eventually, if they don't replace these chains, one will break and the whole thing will come down on the heads of the congregation," he reflected.

The Minister of Music took the floor and the praise component of the revival set in. People were standing and waving their arms and shouting.

"Let's take our seats, please," Pastor Mark said as the praise component came to an end.

During the shouting, Jimmy noticed that Kathy had entered through a back door and took a seat next to her mother a few pews in front of him. At the close of the evening, as people filed out of the building, Jimmy walked a few steps behind the widow and her daughter. Suddenly, Kathy's left foot veered out of line on a wet spot on the floor and the girl fell backward and down. Seeing his opportunity, Jimmy rushed forward and took her arm and helped her to her feet.

"I'm the clerk at Hardaway's that helps you and your mother," he said anxiously. "My name is Jimmy Duncan, and I'm mighty pleased to meet you," he managed to say.

Mrs. Peeler looked on approvingly at the young man, and then glanced at Kathy.

"Much obliged for the help up, Jimmy," Kathy said. "I'm proud to make your acquaintance," and then the young girl fell silent.

Feeling satisfied with his actions, the clerk smiled and then excused himself from the two women.

Stuart struggled to walk as he made his way to the main mine shaft. The cramps in his legs were getting worse. After two blocks, he had to stop to catch his breath. A few of the younger miners passed him and took a sideways glance at the gray-haired man.

"He's too old for minin work," a red-haired fellow muttered as he walked by.

No one bothered to stop and ask Stuart if he was well, and by now, they all knew he was not well and would not last much longer with their foreman. Slowly, Stuart began to trudge on and eventually he entered the mine shaft 20 minutes late.

"I want a word with you Duncan," the shrill voice of the foreman was heard to say.

The other miners quickly walked away, leaving Stuart alone with Tommy. Tommy, the foreman, was 22 years old. He was the only man that morning with a high school degree, and he was a good ten years younger than any of his men.

"How do you think you can run that coal cuttin machine today, old man?" Tommy seethed.

"Well sir, I've been runnin it for 40 years and I guess I can do it a bit longer," Stuart said.

"Says, who? A man who can't walk 30 feet and who spits black soot outa his mouth at lunch?" Tommy said. "'You get your coat off that hook and come back with me to the office," Tommy ordered and then walked away.

After his talk with Tommy and the boss, Stuart walked back home. He entered the house and turned the living room light on. He walked over and sat quietly in Linda's rocker. He knew this moment had been on the way now for over a year.   Jimmy, Linda, they would be okay with his not working anymore. They had complained about how harsh the climate below the surface in the mines was. They had seen the effect it had taken on their father's health and the mental anguish he had suffered as all the younger men had ostracized him as someone who was obsolete. There was no community spirit between the younger men and the older men. Men of Stuart's era were considered out-of-touch and fast approaching the point of being useless. Once the older men started to slow down, they were quickly shown the door and told not to come back. Stuart picked up a copy of the Farmer's Almanac and a tear fell down his cheek. His lips trembled. He had never had to depend on anyone and now he couldn't make it by himself. He thought of his long dead wife, who had only known him as a vigorous and strong young man.

"I am not what I once was, and I reckon I better get used to it," he thought.

Linda came home early from her job at the drug store the day Stuart had been let go from the mine.

"Don't say nothin daddy," she whispered, seeing Stuart sitting alone in the rocker. "I already know everything. Marlon called me at noon," she said.

The old man began to stand up from his seat, but Linda softly put her hand on his shoulder.

"Sit yourself down and rest while I start supper," she said.

Stuart could hear Linda singing in the kitchen. Her favorite songs were the old ballads that her Irish grandmother had taught her as a child. Stuart listened to the sounds of kitchen work: the chopping of the large knife on a wooden board, the hissing of steam as it rose from the large kettle of vegetable stew, and the shuffling of his daughter's shoes across the worn floor. It wasn't long until Jimmy came home from the hardware store. The boy sat across from his father and looked into the man's face.

"All your years at the mines brought you nothin but bein throwed out like a cur," he said angrily. "That Tommy is going to get the same as he had given, if'n it's the last thing I ever do," he promised Stuart.

"Now, Jimmy," his father said, "you know what the good book says. We must turn the other cheek and love them that hates us," he said.

"I'm not sure I am up to it, but I know it's our Christian duty," the boy admitted.

The next morning Stuart awoke late. Jimmy and Linda had risen
early and were already at their jobs. Once dressed, he walked to
the kitchen to fix himself a cup of coffee. There he found a meal
waiting for him in a covered dish. Linda had prepared drop biscuits,
two scrambled eggs, and three thick slices of fried ham. As Stuart
chewed, he fancied that Linda's cooking had never tasted better.
He ate two biscuits and put the leftovers in the ice box. After breakfast, despite his failing health, he went outside for a walk in the
streets of his Harlan neighborhood.

The chill of early Spring was in the air as Stuart walked. It had
been a long bitter, cold Winter, but now the worst was over. The
first birds of the season had started settling into the budding trees
of Eastern Kentucky. Stuart walked two blocks down to the river. He stood for a while inspecting the water. Early Spring was
a time of high water. The rushing of the stream had scoured the
banks and eroded the soft earth that washed into the stream and
then made its way downstream to settle on the riverbed. A few
red-headed ducks bobbed about searching for food with their necks
and heads dipping below the surface of the stream. Stuart saw the
body of a dead crow float by.

"I guess that black bird couldn't find enough food," Stuart thought.
"Or maybe it was just sick," he concluded. "When you're a crow
and you're sick, you're just gonna die," he mused. "There ain't
much help for the sick of the animal world," he concluded.

The old man made his way back up the bank of the river onto High
Street, which ran parallel to the stream. He walked along High
Street.

A few blocks along High Street, Stuart stopped in front of a gun
barrel shaped diner. The front window revealed a long narrow bar
along the left side of the interior of the diner. The bar separated the
customers from the cooking area. Along the right side of the diner
interior, across from the bar, were a row of wooden tables with a

few chairs. The diner was poorly lit. Stuart entered and sat in the front behind a large window. There he watched people as they walked along High Street. He ordered brunch.

Within the back of the diner, he could hear two young people talking as they ate.

"You know what Father Bryan tol me," a young male voice related. "Most of this town is on its way to the wrong side of eternity," the voice said. "The Lord makes no exception for them that don't follow his will," the young man related.

"But I'm following his will, Eddie," a female voice pleaded.

"Says who? You mean that idolater with his checkered tie and buck teeth?" The boy said.

"I won't have you sayin that about my preacher, Eddie. He's a god fearin believer," Kathy insisted.

As Stuart listened to Eddie and Kathy argue, he gritted his teeth.

"I know the kind of this Eddie," he muttered. "Him and his Popery are leading him straight to the eternal fire, and that's for sure," the old man thought.

Suddenly, he heard Kathy raise her voice: "you don't know what my momma says agin you Eddie," the girl's voice shook. "She tol me your kind and my kind shouldn't mix, and I better be goin my own way and seein my own people," she said.

Stuart looked up to see the girl walk out the front door alone.

Walking back from the diner, the old man passed by Saint Mary's Church. Saint Mary's was the most opulent building in Harlan.

"This church don't belong here in Harlan," he thought as he stopped in front.

He spat out the black phlegm of his lungs onto the street in front of the church and began walking with his head held down. He thought about what life held in store for him. The mine had been his life, and now that was gone. Most of the men his age that he had worked with were dead or dying.

"I am one of the healthier of my age," he told himself. "I need to get out and walk more: keep the old ticker ticking," he thought.

He slowed his pace to go into his bungalow, and his heart began pounding out of control. He felt fear creep into his mind. He began hitting his chest with his right hand to make his heart slow down. His fist hit his ribs with a force that kept him from feeling his heart pounding. Gradually, the beating of his heart slowed and he entered the house. He took off his shoes and placed them inside the front door. He walked in his socks to the bedroom.

"There ain't much to do now, but get some sleep," he said to himself.

He took his shirt and pants off and got into the metal frame bed and pulled the quilt around him. He soon fell asleep, and after a while he began to dream. In his mind he was back in the mines. Tommy had been really nasty that day, and Stuart felt his anger consume his thoughts as he ran the coal-cutting machine. Before noon, his lantern went out and he was in the dark. He shut off the cutter, got out of the machine and stood up. His eyes peered into the dusty dark of the mine shaft.

Off in the distance, he heard the shouting of the miners: "the vents are plugged and I can't nary catch my breath," he heard.

He then heard the sound of footsteps running along the adjacent mine shaft and then a voice: "we better get outa here while the air is still good, "someone said.

Anxious, he put his hand against the side of the coal shaft and ran it along the wall as he walked toward the entrance. After 20 minutes, his hand couldn't feel the wall and he felt a draft of cold air. At once, something heavy hit him in his side and he fell to the floor of the shaft. At this point Stuart awoke.

Five years went by. Jimmy had quit the hardware store and was working as a mechanic at a local garage. Stuart had convinced his son to attend the local technical school and get his certification as an automotive mechanic. The work at the garage was dirty, but the pay was good. Stuart, Jimmy and Linda needed the extra money. For the first three years, money was tight. The small family barely got by. Then Stuart qualified for Social Security and with Jimmy working at the garage, things were easier. Linda still worked the counter at the drug store, and she and Marlon had been saving up to get married. Marlon had moved out of his rented room and had bought a small place near downtown. It was humble, but Marlon was good with his hands. He, his father, and his two brothers were fixing his place up.

"Kathy and her mom came by the shop today," Jimmy announced at dinner one night.

"I guess that lifted your spirit, Jimmy," Marlon said.

"Could I have some more boiled potatoes," Jimmy said, avoiding the subject.

"I heard from her mother that Eddie gave that Kathy a warnin," Linda mentioned. "He tol her to become Catholic or forget about seein him," Linda mentioned.

"She'll never do that," Jimmy interjected. "She loves the Lord too much to stoop to that," he continued.

"What did the pretty gal and her mom have to say at the shop, Jimmy?" Stuart asked.

"Mrs. Peeler asked for an extension on her account. The cleanin has been slow for them," Jimmy told his father.

"How are they gettin by, Jimmy. What do you think?" Stuart asked.

"Times are hard for them two, like it is for just about everybody in this town," Jimmy answered.

"The Lord will show them the way. He's not gonna turn his back on the faithful," Linda said.

At the garage, Jimmy made good money, but the owner was gruff. He didn't take Jimmy under his wing as Mr. Hardaway had done.

"Have you finished the Ford truck yet?" The owner barked one day.

"No sir, but it is getting there," Jimmy answered.

"I want that thing on the lot in half an hour, got that?" Bob finished and walked back to his office.

After Jimmy had finished the truck, it was lunch time. He was only given 20 minutes for lunch, so he couldn't go out. He brought his lunch and ate it in the back of the garage near the bathroom. As always, the dutiful Linda had packed his food in a paper bag. As he ate, he thought about times wearin on Mrs. Peeler and Kathy. Jimmy had not seen them in a while. Kathy had not been to church with her mother on Saturday nights for several weeks and that concerned Jimmy.

"I hope she has not lost her faith in the church," he worried.

Although Kathy had not been to church much, Jimmy had seen Mrs. Peeler and she had been deferential to the young mechanic.

On Saturday night Jimmy gathered his courage.

'How has Kathy been, Mrs. Peeler?" He asked as church let out.

"Oh, Jimmy, she's a doing poorly," Edna Peeler related. "She and that Eddie broke it off, and the poor gal just sits in her room alone. I talked to her about getting out and mixin, but it aint' doin no good," she said.

"Does she still read the Bible?' The young man asked.

"I am relieved to see her a readin it just about every night," Mrs. Peeler said.

"That's good," Jimmy concluded as he excused himself and walked out into the evening air.

Jimmy walked home since he never drove to the preaching. Once in his room, he took out a large cardboard box beneath his bed and counted out several large bills. He put the bills in his pocket and pushed the box back beneath the bed. He got up and went out into the living room where Stuart and Linda were sitting reading.

"Dad, get this widow and her girl to clean up this place, I am goin to pay," he said.

Stuart looked up. His worn face brightened into a smile.

Since the widow and her daughter did the cleaning of the Duncan home in the mornings, and Jimmy was a work by the time they started, he never saw Kathy when the cleaning was done. But as he worked at the garage, he felt happy knowing that he was helping them. He knew how harsh life in Eastern Kentucky could be. His mind often wandered back to his home, and he imagined the two women at their work. There was the mopping of the floors and the scrubbing down of the walls. Linda paid to have Edna and Kathy do the washing and the ironing. In this way, she could spend more of her time in the evenings with cooking.

One day at work, Jimmy was changing a tire on a truck when the tire exploded. The shock wave from the sudden rush of air knocked Jimmy out. Bob found him on the floor of the garage unconscious.

"Young man, hey Jimmy," Bob said as he tried to rouse the mechanic.

The manner of the usually hard-hearted boss softened and he actually became kind. He sat on the concrete floor with Jimmy's head in his lap and wiped his face with a rag soaked in warm water. Bob called the other men, and they carried Jimmy to the van and drove him to the local emergency room. There the general practitioner examined the boy, who by that time had begun to regain consciousness. The doctor called Bob back into the examining room.

This fella is goin to be okay, just a bad concussion," the doctor said. "Call his sister at the druggist and have him taken home and put in a clean bed," the doctor advised. "And Bob, don't work this man for the next week, or my cousin is comin for you, okay?" He said.

"You got it Doc. Jimmy is off until he can work. You have my promise on that," Bob said.

Jimmy could vaguely hear people moving in the room around him. He tried to open his eyes as he lay in bed, but when he did his vision became blurred. The room seemed dark to him. He could hear Edna Peeler's voice giving directions for cleaning. A metal bucket created a scraping sound as it was being pulled across the floor. He felt a cool towel being placed upon his eyes. He lay half-awake with the pleasant feeling of the wet cloth on his face. He could feel a towel wiping his face and he felt someone take his hand.

His eyes opened and he looked to the side to see a young woman with jet black hair sitting quietly at the bedside. She smiled, but didn't say anything when she saw that he recognized her. Jimmy was filled with a sweet sadness and he began to speak to Kathy.

"Kathy, I haven't seen you at church in a long while and your mother says you have a great sadness," he spoke haltingly. "Kathy, I've been prayin for you, and I want to see you at church again."

The young girl smiled, and her manner became animated and joyful.

"I'll be there Jimmy, but only if you will take me," she said softly.

118

Jerry

Jerry sat at the high-legged table eating his sausage biscuit. He always came to Hardee's the first thing every morning after awakening. This was usually about 5:30 a.m. Jerry was single. He had been divorced for about 20 years and had no plan to remarry. To begin with, a wife was a big expense, and his job at the pest control place didn't pay that well. If you want a quality wife, he had realized, you need more than looks. You need money. Money seemed to be the ticket to a lasting relationship with a pretty young thing. Only 45 years old, he was still fairly attractive. He was slightly taller than average, and he had a lanky, athletic build. Something of a 1960's wanna-be, he wore his long blonde hair tied back into a pony-tail. His face was rugged enough still to be masculine, even with a pony-tail. And the pony-tail seemed to attract progressive, younger women. He usually went for the types that didn't want commitment. In other words, he went for young women pursuing a career by getting an education. These women had put marriage on the back burner. They were only interested in one thing: the thing that Jerry wanted-passion without entanglement.

Jerry looked up from his half-eaten breakfast. His eyes met Angie, the girl behind the counter. Angie was pretty and about 35. She was tall and had dark brown hair and brown eyes. Her complexion was slightly ruddy, as if she were always a bit excited. And she was perky. After all, she spent much of her time flirting with men while she rang up the orders. Although married with two teen-agers at home, Angie had made it clear to Jerry that she was available to him. Jerry frowned as he looked into the dark eyes of Angie.

"Not going there," he muttered, "too complicated," he thought.

Angie's husband, Mat, a mechanic in a county garage, was much bigger than Jerry. Mat had worked over a few of Angie's former lovers. Mat was the jealous type; even though everyone knew that he ran around as much as his buxom wife. Jerry looked down under Angie's stare, feeling the heat rise in his face. He couldn't help pondering Angie's incredibly good looks.

"Not gonna bite," he told himself.

At the pest control service, Jerry's job was to make client visits. This entailed going to the client's home and performing the service of spraying. This morning he pulled his truck up to a modern, stucco home. A middle-aged woman answered the doorbell.

"Back in here," she mentioned as she motioned him toward the bathroom. Once inside the room, he noticed how dirty it was. "Over there," the woman exclaimed pointing toward a corner of the room. Large black roaches were crawling about.

"Don't you ever do any cleaning?" He asked rudely, looking up at the woman as he put his sprayer together.

"Look, just get rid of them," she said.

"I can spray here if you like, but unless you clean this place up, they will come right back," he explained.

"You're a damn liar," the woman said loudly.

Intimidated by her rough manner, and anxious about his payment, Jerry became silent and began the service.

"I think my old man knew you," she said as she watched him work. "Aren't you that guy on the scooter with "lover boy" on the plates?" She asked.

"Yes, that's me. Where did your husband meet me?" He asked her.

"We were downtown at Main Street Pizza, and he saw you get on your scooter. He pointed you out to me," she said. "Don't you own a regular car?" She asked.

Jerry had become nervous with her questions- questions from an older woman he did not know. Without answering, he finished the service and gave her the bill.

"The man of the house will put a check in the mail once he's home," she said, shutting the door in his face.

Saturday night found Jerry at Noonan's. This was his place: a slea-zy eatery and pool hall. Noonan's was located on Main Street in town. Other businesses on Main Street were the vegetarian cafes frequented by the twenty-something crowd and off campus offices of the university. The interior of Noonan's was pine wood paneling with the heads of animals stuffed and tacked to the walls. The out-lying areas around town had not been wilderness for over two-hun-dred years, however, a pioneer lifestyle persisted in the country-side. There women engaging in quarrels sometimes took baseball bats to one another. A fifty-dollar assault charge did not prevent their male counterparts from engaging in a good fight whenever the opportunity presented itself. Jerry leaned against his favorite pool table, Budweiser in hand. Someone had turned the juke box on. A Tammy Wynette song played loudly.

"Hey, cowboy," he heard a female voice say.

He looked over. Laura was a 49 year-old ex-nurse. She had long, bleached blonde hair in a puffed-up style. Her complexion was tanned, and her face was lined by years of hard living.

"Yer lookin mighty fine tonight honey," Jerry drawled as he looked over at Laura with a leer in his eye.

By his inspection, she was a good ten years older than he was, but at this point, he really wasn't thinking age. Laura was one of those older women, who had managed to keep her looks as the years progressed. Her figure could have been taken from the local high school annual, and when it came to taming men she had plenty of experience.

"Rack em up, big boy," Laura said as she leaned down in front of Jerry to chalk up her cue.

Jerry set the rack and the game began. He was very impressed with the manner in which she ran the table. After a few games, Laura came closer to her pool companion, and ran her hand down his thigh.

"I'm getting tired of this honey, "let's split," she whispered close to his face.

Jerry and Laura were soon seen leaving Noonan's together out the back door.

Jerry woke late Sunday still hung over from Saturday night with Laura. From Noonan's they had gone back to her place on the west side of town. He had stayed over and managed to arrive back home Sunday.

"Bout time for a drink," he had told himself alone in his apartment Sunday. Jerry had picked up a two twelve packs of Budweiser at the Road Runner Mart on his way home from Laura's place. By the time he got up Monday morning, the empty cans were strewn about the floor next to his bed.

"Can't make it to Hardees," he had acknowledged to himself as his head throbbed.

He walked to the greasy linoleum counter, next to the gas stove, and boiled water for coffee. In fifteen minutes, he had downed three cups of the strong black brew.

The next week passed quickly. There were plenty of calls for spraying homes in the suburbs. The old white truck barely made it through the work week. One late afternoon, Jerry pulled up to the office in the truck. As he slowed to a stop, a cloud of gray smoke puffed from the tailpipe.

"That ol boss man better come up with cash to keep this thing a goin," he angrily told himself.

Once inside the office he stopped at the front desk. One of the other servicemen was subbing as secretary after Debbie had quit.

"Think to get cash from the calls today?" Fred questioned Jerry looking up.

"Cash? What's that man?" Jerry asked. "I gotta fist full of these checks, and I reckon half of them are bad," he answered with a smirk.

On his way home after work, Jerry pulled his scooter up to the Marathon Gas Station on Oakland Avenue to fill up. He walked slowly inside to pay. The Marathon Station looked old and worn inside. The shelves of the cheap sundries and bags of chips were half empty. The Marathon Station was run by an East Indian couple. The husband had been rude to Jerry, but his wife was always pleasant.

"Fifteen dollars," the Indian woman said quietly looking down at the cash register.

Not one to miss any details where women are concerned, Jerry stood and looked as he pulled out his wallet. She was of medium height and medium build. He noticed that her head had a pretty rounded shape, not slightly flat on the sides like some Western women. The skin of her face was a pale olive, without any blemishes. Her lips, devoid of lipstick, were a delicate coral color.

He tried to catch her eye, but she looked off out the window as she dismissed him with a "have a nice day, today."

The red scooter was the perfect vehicle for around town. It consumed practically no fuel, and it got plenty of attention from pedestrians and other motorists. Most of the blue-collar, single men preferred the big hogs like Harley Davidson. The Harley made plenty of noise and sounded masculine. On the other hand, the hogs were seen everywhere. There was not really anything unique about riding a big bike. The scooter parked easily in the woodshed on the ground floor of Jerry's apartment building.

Jerry had become adept at small bike mechanics and he had learned to fix most of the scooter's problems himself. He had taken a twelve-month course in small gasoline engines at the local community college. In addition, he had been able to keep up its appearance with touch-up paint from Ace Hardware. In the winter, a good leather jacket was all he needed to keep the cold wind at bay.

"I think the scooter may need a new engine," he thought to himself, sitting alone in his apartment on a Friday night.

A quick Google search located a rebuilt engine at a reasonable cost.

"Better than buying a whole new scooter," he realized.

Flipping through "Automotive Mechanics" he dozed off after smoking a few reefers. In the night his dreams reverted to the Indian woman at Marathon Oil. He was at the gas station again and he was standing in line at the check-out. As earlier, she was quietly waiting on the clientele. He notice the refinement of her manners, and the sophistication of the Indian accent as she spoke. His dreamy attention became fixed on her right ear, which was bared by the way her black hair had been pulled back and up into a chignon. Her ear was small and of an olive hue, like the skin of her cheeks. It was finely curved with a shell-like shape. There were small silver rings piercing the olive flesh of her ear. He woke with a start and looked at the plastic alarm clock on the table near his chair in which he had fallen asleep.

"Only two a.m." he muttered.

He rose and began to pace the room. He felt anxious and went to the fridge for another beer. Turning on the portable television set, he spent the rest of the night watching horror movies.

"Great dancers tonight!" Jerry shouted above the din of the band at the local strip show.

An older man standing next to Jerry gave a lecherous grin.

"Which one do you like?" The man asked Jerry in a slightly drunken slur.

"I'll take little blondie over there," was his answer.

"Little blondie" was well-known to Jerry and she was certainly beautiful. She had that delicate, teen-age look, but in truth, she was 33
Sylvia, as her many lovers had known her, had made the rounds
of the married physicians in town. Something of a renegade, she
had turned down marriage proposals from the wealthiest and most
sought-after bachelors in Johnson City. A single Psychiatrist and
notorious lady's man, Dr. Griffin, had become consumed with desire
whenever Sylvia let him near her. She was simply the most provoc-
ative and daring woman in the entire town, and that was the way
she danced on-stage. The woman simply had no inhibitions, but
she did have taste and she did not like Dr. Griffin. Jerry smiled and
slapped his drinking companion on the back.

"I never made it with her," he admitted shouting into his companion's ear. "But it don't matter none to me; there are plenty of gals in
this town," he bragged.

Back in his apartment after the night at the gentleman's club, Jerry
had trouble coming down from the high he had experienced there.
He stumbled to the bathroom and took a few "downers." Soon he
was out for the night. Jerry did not wake up until four a.m the. next
day, which was Saturday. The sky through the open window was
dark and black. He sat in a cane chair, tilted back with the front
legs off the ground and pondered.

"This life is shit, man," he said to himself. "But hell, it's the only life
there is," he concluded.

He thought about his boss, Amos. Amos was abusive and didn't
care to conceal it. He ruled the pest control staff like a dictatorial
high school football coach. Jerry had either been fired or had quit
so many jobs that he knew not to talk back to Amos.

"Ain't no body gonna give me a chance, if I get canned again," he
realized.

His current work life was not that bad as long as he could avoid Amos. Jerry showed up for work early and was on the job well before Amos came to work at 8:30 a.m. Jerry took off late, after Amos had gone home. All he needed to do to get along with his boss is to keep his mouth shut and pick up his check every two weeks. He sat alone watching his plastic clock on the table waiting for five a.m. when Hardees opened.

Just after five a.m. a red scooter swerved in front of a truck on West Market Street. The rider of the scooter seemed distracted to the driver of the truck. Grumbling, the driver revved up the truck to pass the scooter and gave the pony-tailed man the finger as he passed him. Soon, Jerry was at Hardees.

"How ya doin baby doll?" A plump woman behind the cash register drawled at Jerry.

Donna was not the heart breaker that Angie was. She was fifty-ish and rotund. She looked as if she had eaten whole pound packages of margarine as snacks. Jerry looked over, spying Angie's figure at the drive-in window. He could hear her breathy voice as she took an order from a local police officer.

"The usual sausage biscuit," Jerry told Donna, "and by the way...I am not your baby doll...I am too big and mean to be a baby doll," he said to her.

Once at his table, he went to work on the sausage biscuit. A table of rough-looking men in the corner traded news on University of Tennessee football while they watched "Fox and Friends" on the overhanging television. These men did not like Jerry's kind. He looked too sissy. For years the men at the table had been sitting in the corner while Jerry ate. They had not traded a single kind word with him.

"Pretty boys make me sick," one man had told him.

"What do I care? With a stomach like yours, you are lucky to get off the toilet seat in the morning," he had replied.

Jerry did not like "Fox and Friends." The glib talking heads in their designer suits were not his style. He did like the female co-hosts however. The Fox New Network usually managed to hire very attractive women. It was no accident that almost all of the co-hosts were blondes.

"They're in here," a thin woman gesticulated wildly.

"How long have you had ants?" Jerry asked.

"I never had any bugs until the a warm day last week, and now they are all over the place," Sandy used a steel cane to steady herself on her crooked legs.

Jerry took a look at his hostess. At first glance, she looked about 45. Upon closer inspection, he noticed the gray roots near the skin of her scalp. Otherwise, her hair was jet black. Her face was impish, but there were wrinkles about her large green eyes. The skin of her face was drawn taut, belying cosmetic surgery. The real evidence was in her hands.

"I guess this one must be about 68," he said as he followed her back to the kitchen. "Where's your husband?" He asked as he squirted the noxious fluid around the edges of the room.

"Dead!" Sand blurted out. "A dissecting aortic aneurysm,'" she explained. "One minute he was mopping the bathroom floor, and the next minute he was lying on it," she cried. "The EMT couldn't get a pulse or a blood pressure when he arrived. My husband was already cold and blue," she said.

"That must have been a shock," Jerry exclaimed as his eyes in-spected the counter tops for mouse droppings. "I have some ro-dent traps I am gonna leave," he said as he handed a few plastic traps to Sandy.

"Can you stay for cola and pizza?" The woman asked. "I just had a twelve-inch delivered from Fazoli's," she mentioned.

"No ma'am," he grinned. "My girlfriend is expecting me over tonight for her home-made lasagna, and I don't wanna spoil my appetite," Jerry explained.

He quickly loaded up his empty sprayer and made for the door. Once outside, he was gone in an instant.

At the day's end Jerry did not go to his girlfriend's for home-made lasagna. Jerry did not have girlfriends; he had one-night stands. After work, the red scooter winded its way down the lonely street to his place. Once inside his apartment, he opened a twelve-pack of Budweiser. He took the twelve-pack over to his chair next to the table where his plastic clock sat and began drinking. He did not stop drinking until he blacked out.

At some point, he had a vision of being alone in the Marathon Station with the East Indian woman. They were both standing in front of the cash register. She was pressed up against him. He could feel the supple curves of her figure with his body. He reached down and put his arms around her and she gently patted his stomach with her left hand. He didn't have the presence of mind to kiss the woman. He just stood there holding her. She was surrendering to him. As they stood there in this embrace, Jerry was filled with an intense tenderness for her. He hadn't felt like this since the first weeks of his marriage, so long ago.

Jerry awoke the next morning a bit later than usual. He looked over at the plastic clock: six a.m. After the night's binge, he now had the shakes. He felt jittery and nervous. His dream about the Indian woman had disturbed him. He stood upright and his frame wavered. He shook his head to clear his mind, but the same thought kept recurring.

"Why am I so fixated on a married woman, a woman I hardly know?" He thought. "She is not my type," he said to himself. "Commitment and love, that's for the birds," he told himself as he stumbled on unsteady legs to the bathroom.

His hands shook as he opened the medicine cabinet and took out a bottle of Valium. He took two tablets. Jerry returned to bed and lay down waiting for the drug to take effect. He lay with his face to the ceiling. His mind was tense and the excitement of the vision of the foreign woman returned. He felt elated with his memory of her. He remained in this state until 7 a.m. and then he got up to go to work.

Months went by. Jerry made it to Hardees most mornings of the week. Since the night of his drunken vision of the East Indian woman at Marathon Oil, he had been avoiding that gas station.

"After all," he told himself, "what was the point of hanging around this woman? Sure, she was a rare beauty, but there were a lot of other fish in the sea," he said to himself.

After a few more months, he began driving by the Marathon Station in the evenings. He never went in and he didn't buy gas there.

"The Marathon gas is really not up to par," he thought.

Jerry had decided the woman's rude husband had allowed ground water to seep into the gas tanks at the Marathon Station. He had convinced himself that the sputtering of the scooter was the result. Despite buying gas at Exon and Shell, however, the sputtering continued.

"I think that with these other gasolines, the sputtering is getting better," he said to himself one night.

As was his habit, during the university's winter and spring terms, he had been picking up lonely coeds from the bars for the night. As a precaution, he had made an appointment with his primary care doctor to get checked for sexually transmitted diseases. The other men he knew with low paying jobs, relied on the coeds as well. They all made regular visits to their medical providers as a precaution also. After one particularly bad day at work, Jerry did not make it to work the next day. He had left a voice mail on the office phone. He reported over the phone that he was coming down with the flu. It was winter by that time and flu season was in full force.

"I know the office will believe me," he promised himself.

That night the East Indian woman had appeared to him in a dream again. During the dream, he had entered the Marathon Station and walked to the back of the store to get a Dr. Pepper and Snickers bar. As he approached the Indian woman at the checkout, she was turned slightly away from him, revealing her well-molded shoulders and neck. He could only see the side of her face. The shape of her delicate chin and cheek was unmistakable. As the customers in front of him left, he stood directly in front of her. Suddenly, she looked up at him and her dark eyes made contact with his eyes. He felt in the dream as if there were a secret message being exchanged between the woman and him. At this point, he was roused from sleep by the jangling of the plastic clock.

"Dammit," he cursed. "I have stayed away from her for too long. It won't do no harm just to go by and see how she looks today," he told himself. "I think she is just the ticket to cheer me up," he thought as he climbed onto the scooter.

The Marathon Oil Station was several miles away from his apartment, so as he puttered his way there, he felt his spirit lift. The gray clouds did not seem so gray, and the cold air felt warmer. As he approached the station, he recognized the dull blue paint of the store front and the familiar advertisements for LOTTO cards that were in the window. His heart began to race as he grasped the door handle and walked insided.

"Can I help you sir?" A young East Indian boy asked.

Jerry's head turned in the direction of the boy and he stared at him. The boy was thin, with an oversized head and short, clipped hair. The clerk's eyes protruded and he had a frayed shirt with plastic writing pens in his front shirt pocket. The boy smiled widely displaying poor dentition. Confused, Jerry felt as if he were about to lose balance. Without answering the clerk, his eyes quickly searched the store for the beautiful woman he had come to see. Behind him, tacked above the door as he turned, was his answer: a large sign was posted with the words: NEW MANAGEMENT printed in large letters.

Jack

Jack stood at the front of the board room, "the quarterly results are promising gentlemen," he said. "The project in Nigeria is on schedule. We have cut a deal with the local government to operate largely tax free. Labor laws are virtually nonexistent and there is an endless supply of hard-scrabble manpower," he concluded.

The Board of Directors looked on approvingly at one another and many in the room were in agreement.

"But how has the share price fared?" Queried Dick Smothers, a majority shareholder and activist investor.

"Well, we have beat the average in the broader market indices. So I would say we are well ahead of the game this fiscal year," Jack responded.

It was near the end of the two-hour presentation required by the Board of Directors, and Jack was relieved. He had staved off another session of out-of-control investor demands and remained on top as the CEO of Wellcorp, one of the big three in the crude oil and refinement industry.

The executive suite of Wellcorp was on the sixty-fourth floor of the Chicago Trade Center. The decor was modern and spare, somewhat reminiscent of a Scandinavian design. Jack occupied the corner office with a wide-angle view of the downtown skyline. At the entrance to the executive suite, the departmental assistant was stationed. Sherry was a 24 year-old graduate of business school and had initially started at Wellcorp as a temp. The workday began promptly at 7:30 a.m. with the executive briefing session five days per week. All vice-presidents attended along with Jack, the chief executive officer.

When Sherry accepted a permanent position at Wellcorp, the job seemed glamorous. But she soon found out, that came with a cost: the pay was abysmal and the other support staff were witchy. To compensate for the low salary, she bought all of her clothes at Pen-

ny's. Her efficiency apartment, located in one of the seedier neigh-
borhoods near downtown, was within the shadow of impressive,
high-rise buildings. This made traveling to and from work more
cost-efficient, since she could be at her desk within 20 minutes of
leaving her apartment. Her Geo Metro car was perfect for a single
woman. Its five-cylinder lightweight engine did not consume much
gasoline, and the small size of the vehicle could accommodate
even the smallest of parking spaces. This obviated the need to rent
an expensive space in a nearby, for-profit parking garage.

Within four blocks of the Wellcorp building, downtown changed
dramatically: 50 to 80 story modern, high-rise buildings were replaced by older brick buildings from four to six stories high. These
older residential buildings averaged 100 years in age, having been
built in the early twentieth century. They were erected during years
of immigration from Eastern Europe just after the end of the first
World War. The people who lived there now were a mix of recent
arrivals from the Middle East and South America in addition to entry
level employees of the downtown corporations. There was a pleth-
ora of immigrant groceries and restaurants in the area. Within a
few blocks of Sherry's apartment, one could find the local Catholic
Church and mosque. One a good day, Sherry walked everywhere.
In the neighborhood she found everything she needed for single
life: groceries, a laundry, and a local yoga studio where she worked
out and met other young adults.

Sherry had lived in the same apartment since attending business
school. Before that, she had lived at home while working part-time
as a model. She was a bouncy blonde with Madison Avenue looks,
and she was a favorite at the agency where she worked. She had
the elegance required of models of clothing and perfume advertisements. Sherry switched off the portable television set. She stared
at the lead gray of the cathode ray tube as stories of political and
corporate corruption receded from her consciousness. The sound
of a heavy truck making its way through the street below could be
heard through the cloth curtains. She had put plastic backing on
the curtains herself to block out the glare of the street night lamps,
but the sounds of the street at night were not obscured. Her gaze
fell on the brown paint of the cabinet above the sink, and she
thought of home-made biscuits. Walking across the single room of

her efficiency apartment, she began searching through the shelves for a tin cannister of enriched flour. Prying the top off the cannister, she reviewed its nearly empty contents.

"Time to visit the Raza family next door," she thought.

Five minutes later she was standing in the hall dropping the metal door knocker onto its strike plate. Sobia answered. Sobia was the wife of Rafi, a Pakistani graduate student. They lived in the apartment next to Sherry. Sobia and Rafi had three children, all under six years of age. The youngest, Mona, could be seen behind Sobia running around in diapers. The little girl was just over a year old in age and was mastering the art of walking unattended. The humidity of the apartment greeted Sherry as Sobia smiled and waved at her from inside.

"Sobia, I need some of your flour for biscuits," she explained.

"Nonsense, darling," Sobia answered, "you must stay for dinner," she said.

Behind Sobia and Mona, the two other children and Rafi were sitting around a large family table. Soon all were seated and the evening meal began. The Raza's had introduced Sherry to Mediterranean cuisine. They partook of tabooli, lamb shishkabob, and a variety of fruits. Periodically, they would wrap pita bread around a spoonful of hummus and wash everything down with water.

The conversation at the Raza table centered on the lives of their Pakistani family. Rafi's father had been a dealer of live chickens for slaughter. He had sent his sons to college in Karachi. As soon as the boys were of age, the senior Raza had sponsored them in graduate schools in American universities. Rafi's two brothers were currently living in New York. Before completing the Graduate Record Examination and being accepted to Graduate School, Rafi had worked as a high school biology teacher in the Bronx.

Rafi was currently working on his PhD in genetics at the University of Chicago. Sobia had a degree in Middle Eastern Antiquities, and had married Rafi in the usual arranged marriage soon after graduating from college. As the evening wore down, Sobia walked Sherry to the door with Mona hanging around her legs. Sherry retreated to her apartment with a tin of stone ground wheat flour.

Jack poked at the chicken crusted with cashews with his fork.

"Well," Nancy began, "the girls at the club are in favor of the Tudor house on Bristol Avenue. After all, each of the kids should have their own bedroom with a walk-in closet and bath. Patsy has insisted that she and Dan move to the west side where all the newest construction is being built," she said.

Jack looked up at his wife. Her hair was arranged in the most becoming fashion. Her eyebrows were elegantly tapered, and her nails benefited from only the best manicurist.

His mind wandered back to the office, while Nancy continued: "but really, I don't think the members of our new club have the class that comes with old money. Everything there is so...Gosh! Oh, and I know that you don't like Saint Croix, but I need a rest and I have booked three rooms at the Marriott for two weeks over Christmas. I knew you wouldn't mind. Josh and Sarah will be off from college and we can all have a nice time," Nancy said as she smiled pertly.

After dinner, Jack retreated to his den. There he turned on the flat screen TV and began watching "Wall street Week" with Louis Rukeyser. He sat listening to the financiers from New York review the latest financial news. Picking up his cell phone, he dialed a number.

"Jack dear," a voice responded, "I thought it was still dinner time for you and Nancy," the woman said.

"You know how that goes, Carol," he mumbled, "between courses I found out that I will be in Saint Croix with her and the kids for two weeks over the holidays," he finished.

"Ugh," Carol exclaimed, "I know how you hate that place, but the little woman must have her way," Carol said.

"What are you doing Saturday about one-ish?" He asked.

"I tell you what," Carol replied, "meet me at El Capitan's and we can have a nice lunch," she said.

"Done," Jack answered with authority.

"See you, honey, good to go," Carol replied and then she hung up.

Carol was a young executive at Wellcorp. She and Jack met on a corporate trip to Indonesia three years before. In Indonesia, they had hit if off instantly. She had a trim runner's figure and a mind as sharp as her fashion sense. She and Jack had spent hours at an Asian noodle shop in Jakarta hashing over the issues of life. Since then, there had been a number of convenient get-togethers. Her office in Chicago was conveniently located on the north side of the city near the lake.

"She is really great," Jack smiled to himself with satisfaction.

Jack walked slowly back to the large bedroom which he shared with Nancy. She was at the vanity completing her nightly toilette. With her hair pinned back and after donning silk pajamas, she pulled the wool comforter about her five-foot five frame and soon she was fast asleep.

While Nancy slept, Jack stayed awake lying next to her. His mind was whirling. The Nigeria project had been stalled for two years. A coup had been attempted upon the authoritarian government by Islamic rebels. This had disrupted the tax system of Nigeria and the package of perks that Wellcorp had negotiated from the President of Nigeria. Well-placed bribes from a number of Wellcorp executives had stabilized the situation somewhat, but there was still reason to worry.

Jack reflected. Nigeria had been an unexpected trove of crude oil, but the oil was back in the jungle. Transportation by large trucks over narrow tree-lined roads made things challenging. On the other hand, the Nigerian port was well-equipped to accommodate even the largest oil tankers that came into port. The port had been built by the Chinese, but a simple phone call from the Chairman of the Board of Directors had convinced the Nigerian President to nation-alize the facility. The stress of his job at Wellcorp had given Jack a healthy case of insomnia. Midnight found him pondering the latest corporate bond offerings before he slipped off to sleep.

Sherry's eyes were fixed on Jack's neatly trimmed nails as he gath-ered the morning's executive briefing folder.

'Thanks gal," he said as he made his way to the Board Room past Sherry's desk.

She followed the executive's figure as he walked away. Jack was young for a chief executive officer. At 48, he was at least ten years junior to any of the vice presidents. He was of medium height, had short blonde hair and was on the wiry, thin side. His face was not particularly handsome, but his whole demeanor displayed the power and strength of will it took to manage a major corporation. In Sherry's view, Jack's attention was more desirable than any of the vice presidents. His manner to her was formal, but considerate, and he took the time to smile pleasantly her way each morning. She bent over a large stack of mail and hunkered down to the work of the day.

Noon found Sherry in the break room at the end of the hall. Ev-eryone of the support staff at Wellcorp brown bagged it for the noonday meal. An assortment of secretaries and clerks sat togeth-er. The room was somewhat bare of furniture besides the single plastic-topped table and the metal folding chairs. Large windows on the outer side of the room radiated the cold temperatures of the air outside the building. Nearer the center of the room, away from the door, the warm air of the central heating system wafted over the staff as they ate.

"I don't mind saying it but that Nancy is a bitch," reflected Donna, who was Jack's personal secretary. "This morning she barged right past my desk, without any permission, and cornered Jack in his office. And he was in the middle of a conference call with New York. But that is nothing to the likes of her," Donna said.

Nancy was well known to the staff. Unlike her husband, who treated everyone with respect, Nancy was hostile and condescending to the employees. That morning she had given Jack the same treatment.

"What is the meaning of this?" Nancy dropped a residential sales contract onto the desk in front of her husband.

Jack looked down and turned over the pages with his right hand. He knew the contract. It had arrived special delivery addressed to him with Nancy's signature affixed. The document was an offer to buy the three-story Tudor that Nancy liked. Jack had refused to co-sign the contract and had sent it back to the Realtor along with an angry phone call.

"I will have this house, you'll see," Nancy announced as Jack swiveled his chair to face the window and grimly surveyed the Chicago skyline.

Defeated for the moment, Nancy had stalked from the room and had given Donna a spiteful look as she left.

It was Saturday, 1:20 p.m. at El Capitan's. Jack sat alone at a corner table. There was a light touch from a hand on his shoulder. He looked around; it was Carol.

"Carol!" He exclaimed and he stood up.

She greeted him with a hug, and he helped her into her chair.

"What are you having today?" He asked.

"The burrito supreme here is pretty good, but I am trying to go Vegan so I think I will have the vegetarian fajitas." She answered. Carol reached out with her right hand and laid it on his forearm. "How are Josh and Sarah?" She asked.

Jack took a moment to reflect. "Sarah is doing great at Northwestern. She just returned from a year of study abroad at Cambridge. I am so proud," he said. "The boy, on the other hand, is something to worry about. I had to fly to Gainesville last semester and revoke his credit cards. That didn't go over very well with Nancy," he said.

Carol got misty-eyed and looked over Jack's shoulder. "Josh is so cute," she said.

Jack frowned, "cute is not going to go far in the real world, and I think you know that as well as I do," he said.

"But daddy is there to make things right, isn't he?" She asked.

"Not really, I am there less and less these days. Especially since Josh just failed ten out of fifteen credit hours last semester. I've half a mind to cancel the tuition checks. I think a few months of working the counter at Burger King might set things straight. But then, there is Nancy. When it comes to Josh, she can be a real problem," Jack said.

"From what I heard happened in your office the other day, that is not the only problem with Nancy," Carol giggled.

Jack and Nancy met when Jack was in the MBA program at Loyola University. He had dropped out of medical school at Northwestern during his third year. In medical school, grades were not his problem. He had managed to pass all of his preclinical courses during the first two years. Jack's first semester of his third year he was on the cancer ward as a clinical clerk in Internal Medicine. The agonizing deaths of the cancer patients had unnerved him. He knew he did not have what it took to be a physician. He had majored in business as an undergraduate, so he enrolled in the Graduate

School at Loyola. Nancy was a freshman English major when they met at the student center grill on a Sunday afternoon. Jack proposed when Nancy got pregnant with Sarah. Jack's father, the chief of Personnel at Wellcorp, had supported his son through graduate school. Then he helped him get his foot in the door at Wellcorp.

The second quarter of the fiscal year had not gone well for Jack. After seven consecutive quarters of growth, things at Wellcorp had crashed. There had been an oil refinery explosion in Indonesia, and an oil tanker had capsized off the coast of Nigeria. Dick Smothers, chairman of the Board of Directors was livid.

"What are you going to do about the share price now, mister?" He had asked Jack with challenge in his voice.

With the two disasters, investors had been spooked and "buy" orders were off. The price of Wellcorp stock had plummeted.

"Gentlemen, we will come back from this," was Jack's reply. "I have given Frank his notice in Indonesia and he will be moved out of his office today," Jack promised.

"But that leaves the Jarkarta office without leadership," Dick had complained.

"Furthermore, to boost profitability, I have ordered a ten percent reduction in the white-collar staff at the North-shore office," Jack replied. "Do the math, gentlemen, these two actions will add millions to the balance sheet," he said.

"We'll see," Dick replied. "This better damn well work," he snorted.

After the meeting, Jack was shaken. He knew his career depended on a quick turnaround of events. He gathered his papers and left the boardroom. As Jack passed Sherry's desk, she couldn't help but notice the pained expression on his face. She closed her desk drawer and made for the break room.

As Sherry passed the CEO's office, she paused and glanced inside. Jack was sitting with his front to the door, head down and his face buried in his hands. A young woman with long wavy brown hair was sitting next to him with her head on his shoulder. It was Donna. Sherry immediately continued to the break room and sat down. Except for Sherry the break room was empty. She struggled to make sense of what she had just seen. She knew about Jack's meeting with the Board of Directors. The intercom had been turned on at her desk and she had heard the entire meeting.

After about 40 minutes, the door to the break-room slowly opened and Donna came in, sitting right next to Sherry. Donna's mascara was streaked from crying. She poured out her heart to Sherry, telling her everything about Jack and her in his office. Donna had been Jack's personal secretary for the six years he had been Wellcorp's youngest chief executive officer. Donna and Jack were close, but Donna was happily married to a mechanic and they had two children. Despite her feelings for Jack, Donna was an honest woman. The two women shared that all they could do was work hard and be supportive of the people they cared about. This was the only way they could cope with the downturn in the affairs at the corporation. Each one swore to the other that she would continue on.

It was six o'clock on a Friday evening and the jazz clubs of Chicago were just starting to turn up the music for the evening. The clubs would not close until at least two a.m. the next morning. Sherry picked up her cell phone and made a call.

"Hey, I thought it was you," answered Jake. "I'm right on time, and I will be at your door in 45 minutes," he said.

"Uh, that's what I'm calling you about Jake. You see, I just threw up the burritos I brought home from the office. I've been in bed for 20 minutes," Sherry explained.

"Man," Jake exclaimed. "I guess it can't be helped," he finished.

"I'm really sorry Jake," Sherry replied. "I'll see you next week, okay?" She said.

"Sure," Jake replied and then hung up.

Sherry made her way to her clothes closet and chose a becoming leotard and top. She pulled on a faux tiger fur coat, grabbed her yoga mat and headed toward the door. Soon she was outside of her apartment and walking hurriedly along the slanted and uneven sidewalks of the city. The night's activity surrounded her. Pubs and other eateries were welcoming their guests for the evening. Customers were buying food from the all-night groceries and people were out on the walkways.

After five blocks of walking, Sherry stopped at an exterior doorway between a barber shop and a bar. She climbed two flights of stairs and entered the third-floor landing. At a door to the right of the stairwell, she swiped a magnetic card and entered the studio of Hot Yoga. The air was warm and humid, and most of the other yogis were already present. There were about fifteen Hispanic and Middle Eastern women and two slender young men. The women were between 20 and 40 years of age, and they were predominantly young mothers and divorcees. Sherry greeted those she knew and waved to Judy, the yoga instructor. Judy was about 50, but remarkably trim for her age. She had a teased-out hairstyle, much larger than the size of her face. She was a full-time disc jockey at Chicago 57 and taught yoga two nights per week.

The evening at Hot Yoga began with a series of Yin style asanas and then progressed to a variation of the Sun Salutations. The lesson ended with a few "power" yoga handstands. The last ten minutes of the class were spent in the "death pose." After the session, Sherry felt a tug on her sleeve. It was Sobia.

"Hey, girl," Sobia laughed. "I see you couldn't stay a minute longer in that dive of yours," she said.

Sherry grinned, "Ya, it's not luxury that I am living in," she said.

"How about a quick veggie sandwich?" Sobia pleaded.

"Let's," agreed Sherry.

On the street it was only a twelve-minute walk to the Bronx Deli. They entered and sat at a table near the window.

Munching on a cucumber sandwich, Sobia asked, "how's Jake?"

"That's a sore topic, honey," Sherry replied. "We've only been see-ing each other three months and already he wants to move into my place," Sherry said.

"Whoa, that's too heavy, girl," Sobia crowed. "Really, Sherry, is this guy going anyplace?" Sobia asked.

"No way," Sherry moaned. "Six months ago he dropped out of Loyola and now his is working at FED/EX Kink O's" she related. 'Frankly," she finished, "I canceled out date tonight. Can you blame me?" She said.

"Hardly, young one," Sobia concluded. Sobia took a quick swig of lime juice and bragged: "Rafi has gotten good evaluations from the grad school faculty. I think he can make it all the way. But the kids, they can drive you up a wall. Mona is learning to talk and the only words she knows are "no" and 'shut up," Sobia said.

Sherry and Sobia looked through their purses for any extra change they might have. Together they came up with 20 dollars, and they placed the money under their plates as a gift for the waitress. Talking excitedly, the two friends walked back to their apartments.

"Donna, could you come in here for a minute?" Jack switched off the intercom and began to dictate a letter.

Dick Smothers
Majority Shareholder
Wellcorp

Dear Sir:

Since the onset of the downturn at Wellcorp, equities have made a tremendous rebound. The origin of the explosion at the refinery in Jakarta has been identified: an explosive intermediate in the refining process of crude oil is the culprit. The chemists have altered the process to put an end to this intermediate. On the Nigerian front, the criminal court of Nigeria has convicted the chief pilot of the tanker that went down of criminal negligence. He is now incarcerated for, hopefully, quite some time. In addition, we have terminated the contract with the tanker company and have written a new merchant marine contract with their competitor. I hope this assuages your concerns. I expect further improvement in the share price over the next four quarters.

Sincerely,
Jack Steward

Chief Executive Officer

"I want to visit daddy," Nancy quipped.

It was Sunday afternoon, several months after Jack's bad meeting with the Board of Directors. Over the years, he had developed a dislike of Nancy's father, and this had deepened since her father's stroke. Nancy's mother had been dead for a number of years, and the old man was living in a stroke rehab center in Champaign, Illinois. Once Jack and Nancy were in the car, the long drive out of the city began. The Illinois countryside was boring, Jack reflected. Miles of flat cornfields passed with the hours. Thirty minutes outside of Champaign, Jack and Nancy pulled up to a 24-hour Stuckey's rest stop. Jack gassed up, and then he went inside the blue-roofed store. Returning to the car, he got in and started the engine.

"Here," he said as he tossed on of Stuckey's famous pecan logs to Nancy.

One p.m. found them parking at the rehab center in town.

Nancy and Jack sat down by Nancy's father. They had found him sitting in a wheelchair near a window with a blanket over his lap and legs. Mr. Dowd had not been able to talk since the stroke, but his daughter was convinced that he understood every word that was said to him. Nancy chatted about her early life as a child in Champaign. Mr. Dowd looked up and smiled. He opened his mouth whenever his daughter brought a spoonful of applesauce near his lips. She fed him his lunch, which had been placed on a table on wheels. A partially paralyzed hand pulled incessantly at the edge of the blanket on his lap. After lunch, Nancy brushed his hair while Jack sat silently nearby.

Walking back to their car after the visit, Nancy reflected. "Daddy looked well, don't you think honey?" She said. Jack nodded. "I think he really enjoyed my story about the pony he bought me when I was in high school," she said. "He does seem a bit stronger. I don't believe that he will never talk again. Those doctors don't know everything. Really, some of them think that they are God," she said with exasperation.

As Jack drove his wife back to Chicago, he couldn't help but resent Nancy's father. The old man had run out of money and Jack had picked up all the bills. And her father didn't seem anywhere near death. The neurologist had told his anxious wife that some patients lived on for years even after very serious strokes. After three hours, the Chicago cityscape loomed before them. Nancy had fallen asleep, and Jack's mood began to recover from the gloom of the rehab center and its chronically ill inhabitants.

Months went by, and Sobia had not seen much of Sherry. Occasionally, they would meet between the two apartments. There were always friendly greetings. Sobia had spent the afternoon cooking. She had been rolling out the thin philo pastry for baklava as she was busy preparing the evening meal. Along with the pastry she had prepared chopped walnuts with wild honey. In addition she had chopped up lamb and garlic for shishkabob. Cucumbers, tahini sauce and hummus with pita bread would complete the evening meal.

Mona had been irritable that day, often clinging to Sobia's skirt. She had been running a fever, had a runny nose and she had been coughing. Sobia had taken her to the Pediatric Clinic that morning and had made a stop by the local drug store on the way home. The two other children were in kindergarten. Taking Mona by the hand, Sobia walked to the local preschool and collected Shereef and Ahmed. Returning, the four of them climbed the stairs to the third floor landing, and by that time Rafi was home.

"Rafi, dear, I need to take Ayesha some of the baklava." Sobia announced at the conclusion of their evening meal.

"Sobia, take her some of the hummus and pita bread as well," Rafi replied.

Sobia wrapped her veil around her face and headed out. Ayesha was a friend from the Mosque. She worked as a waitress three blocks from Rafi and Sobia's apartment. It was a cold walk that evening to Ayesha's place of employment. The wind blew Sobia's skirt beneath her tightly buttoned jacket. It had rained earlier in the day and puddles of water lay in the depressions and cracks of the sidewalk. Spying the lights of Jeremy's Pub, Sobia entered in high spirits. As she walked to the server's station, she saw Sherry and an older man siting at a small round table. Sobia could not catch Sherry's eye. The man was perhaps 50 or so, with short blonde hair and commanding manner. Sherry seemed deferential and shy with him.

"Ayesha, do you know that couple?" Sobia asked. As she unwrapped her gift of food.

"Oh, yes," was the reply. "But I don't ask any questions," Ayesha said. "They have been regulars here for about three months. The girl seems too young for him, and you know, he has a big gold ring on his left hand-married," Ayesha informed Sobia.

The next Saturday evening, Sherry found herself alone at eight
o'clock. Jack had not called that week. She unrolled her yoga mat
and began to meditate with her face turned to the window and the
night outside. Incense was burning on a plate on the chest of draw-
ers, and the light from the desk lamp was turned low. There was a
knock at the door and Sherry rose to answer. Opening the door,
she spied Sobia's short, plump figure.

"Girl, I must come in," Sobia said with urgency.

Sherry noticed the distress on her neighbor's face. They sat facing
one another on the couch.

"What is it?" Sherry asked Sobia.

Sobia hesitated and looked at Sherry and them mumbled in con-
fusion: "that man you were with last week at Jeremy's. Oh, Sherry
dear, this is not good at all," she said with alarm.

Sherry's countenance fell and she looked down into her lap.

"Child, what can a married man give you but lies and secrets you
cannot share with anyone?" Sobia asked.

Sherry's lip began to quiver, and she then spoke in a trembling
voice. "Sobia...I'm lonely...So very lonely and miserable," she said.
Sherry felt small and weak.

"And haven't I been lonely and so sad I could cry until I finally met
Rafi?" Sobia replied emphatically. "You cannot give up this early
in your life. You are very young. I am begging you, dear one, give
this man up...You must," she said and Sobia gave Sherry a hug.

Sherry's arms felt limply at her side.

Two weeks later Sherry was in the break room. She was de-
pressed and scared. After Sobia had left her apartment the night
of her visit, Sherry had not slept much. The door to the break-room

suddenly opened and Donna entered in a frantic state.

"Sherry, I heard it all on the intercom: Jack has been fired," Donna said.

Sherry listened, already numb to anything that was happening around her.

Donna then raised her voice. "There was an investigation into Jack and this woman-Carol-from the North-shore office.. It was delivered to Dick Smothers last week, and you know how that man hates Jack," she said. "Get up and come with me," Donna insisted.

The two friends entered the hall. Jack had already been escorted off the premises. Many of his staff were standing around silently. No one had anything to say.

After Jack's termination as CEO, things in the executive suite at Wellcorp were not good. No one was happy to see the fall of such a young and promising man. Word trickled down the corporate pipeline that, although he was finished as CEO, he was being re-tained and would be sent to the Jakarta office. Donna wondered if Nancy would follow her husband to a third world dead-end, or bail out of the marriage to stay in Chicago. Jack had been abandoned by all of his friends in the city. His parking spot in the Wellcorp ga-rage had been reassigned.

Nancy and Jack sat alone in the penthouse, now up for sale. The shock of her husband's infidelity still fresh, Nancy had grabbed him forcefully pulling his shirt sleeve.

"Why?" She had shrieked.

He did not answer, but just stared into space.

"Really, what is there to say?" He had admitted to himself.

He tried to rationalize that everything was Nancy's fault; her and her upwardly mobile dreams of being a socialite. But he knew that was a lie. He had become complacent with marriage, and a man with influence and prestige is never lacking for available mistresses.

"By some miracle, Nancy is still sleeping in the same bed with me here in this apartment," he thought.

The evening dragged on in silence. Jack didn't notice when his tired wife finally went to bed. He tried to watch television, but couldn't. He trudged to the bedroom, took off his clothes and climbed into the bed. He turned over and looked at his wife. She inched her slender fingers next to him. Her hand brushed against his. Jack began to relax and fell asleep.

Elena

Elena stood at the counter and ordered lunch. An onlooker could tell that she was once a very beautiful woman. She was tall and with a very fair complexion. Her skin had a soft and supple look. But now, nearing 30, her face appeared careworn. Still, the curve of her chin and the shape of her nose were becoming. She sat down to eat. She looked down listlessly. Life had not been kind to Elena. Her only marriage had ended suddenly, five years before. She had no idea where her former husband lived. In fact, she did not care where he lived. Her clothes were humble. Elena shopped at the second-hand clothing stores. She chose her items carefully. Something of a non-conformist, her light brown hair was colored a bright turquoise. She had applied the dye herself, having purchased it at a local drug store. Fingering the brown paper bag, she took out a hamburger and large French fries and began to eat. Elena did not drink soft drinks. She only drank water, and she preferred to have it iced, even in Winter. It was cold outside the diner. The early winds of September had given the air a chill. Inside the diner, it was a bit warm, she thought.

An older gentleman watched Elena with interest. He wanted to go over and talk to her, but he could not tell if she wanted company. She looked aside at him and then glanced back at her food. There was no emotion on her face inviting him into her world. He mused about her. He thought she looked unhappy. He could not have known that she worked down the street for a Mexican couple at their family Latino grocery.

The gentleman was older; he was 62. He was married, but his wife had been sick for years. He loved his wife and had always been faithful to her. Even so, he yearned for the companionship of a woman like Elena.

"The gold ring on my finger might get in may way," he thought, even though he had no intention of pursuing romance with the woman in the corner-Elena with the turquoise hair. He walked slowly toward her, trying to catch her eye. She made a hasty exit for the door, seeing that this older man showed an interest in her.

"What is his angle? They all have an angle," she thought as she walked to her sedan.

Elena drove home from the diner. It was Saturday. Once inside her small apartment, Otis approached her and rubbed against her leg. Elena reached down to give him a back rub. Otis was Elena's nine-year-old cat. He was diabetic and shed hair horribly. The vet bills had been expensive, but she had come through whenever Otis needed her. Since her marriage had ended, she had avoided men. There was always some paunchy blue-collar man interested in Elena. After all, despite her age, she had maintained a somewhat trim figure. The country club style of man avoided her. Her plain clothes and off-beat hairstyle scared them off.

"Fancy men probably think I am a street-walker," she said to herself as she dished out a high-fiber, diabetic friendly meal to Otis.

Elena sat down and called Beth.

"You won't believe what happened to me at the diner," she related.

"Don't tell me it's that police guy," Beth moaned.

"No, Jim wasn't there, and I am so relieved. You know he gives me the creeps; he and his obsession with crime. I have told him over and over that I am just not interested in men anymore," Elena complained.

"That's you and me too," Beth chimed in. "They are so needy, always needing a shoulder to cry on," Beth continued.

"And then there are there physical needs, Beth," Elena said, "you know that is all they think about. At the diner today this old guy kept looking at me, and I didn't even look back," Elena told Beth.

"What did he look like girl?" Beth asked.

"He was major handsome," she told her friend.

"You know it doesn't matter what they look like," Beth told Elena. "Did you think he wanted to talk to you?" Beth asked.

"I couldn't tell," Elena said. "He kept looking down at his soft drink and then he would sneak a peak at me," Elena bragged. "I thought about giving him a smile, you know, just to brighten his day. But that might give him the wrong idea about who I am," she said.

"My ex called me last night and chewed me out," Beth told Elena.

"What was that all about?" Her friend asked.

"Does there have to be an explanation? I am about the cut him off, but he does come in handy when I need him," Beth said.

"Don't turn down help if you need it," Elena advised. "This town is mean enough," she explained.

After the two friends hung up, Elena was alone. This was the usual condition that she found herself in on the weekends.

"Alone suits me just fine," she said to herself.

With nothing special to do, she laid down on her bed and pulled the blanket over her fully-clothed body. Thoughts of her failed marriage began to make their way into her consciousness. The marriage lasted only six weeks. All six weeks had been bad. On their honeymoon to Myrtle Beach, Ed had been difficult.

"Why do you have to buy these old clothes? They embarrass me," he had blurted out over dinner.

Not wanting to start a fight, she had not answered him. When the weather had turned unseasonably cold, he had refused to buy her a sweater.

"I am not a money pit," he had told her. "You have a sweater and it's not my fault that you did not bring it along," he had said.

Back in Greeneville, soon after the honeymoon, he just stopped talking. He was sullen. He would come home from the farm supply store and start drinking. Elena did not drink.

"It is bad for you," she had told Ed.

"Look, just don't tell me what to do," Ed had told Elena.

Elena woke to hear the cell phone ringing. It was Sunday morning around ten o'clock.

"Hello," she mumbled.

"It's me, are you still in bed?" Her mother said. "Aren't you going to church today, honey?" Sally pleaded. "You know what your father would think if he knew that you just don't go," her mother emphasized.

"I'm not going anymore," Elena said. "I can't sit in the pew and ignore the collection plate; I am so outa cash," she said. "You know how things have gone for me. Don't tell dad," she pleaded. "You know he tried to die until I got myself saved," she finished.

"What do you expect, Elena? After all, the church is his chosen profession," her mother explained.

"I may go next week, but don't nag me about it," Elena insisted. "Listen mom, Beth called me earlier and we're going to Haven of Mercy for a few clothes. Want to join us?" She asked.

"Honey, I know you like those places, but I wouldn't want any of the church members to see me there," her mother related.

Beth and Elena rummaged through the sweaters laying out on the tables at the Haven of Mercy, Sunday afternoon. With Elena's turquoise hair and Beth's orange hair, the two women added color to the stores at which they shopped. Beth picked up a clean white sweater and held it up.

"What do you think?" She asked Elena.

"Why did you do it, Beth?" Her friend asked.

"What? It is a pretty good sweater," Beth complained.

"No, I mean, why did you just walk out on him? You two were so good together," Elena said.

"Look sister, how good can things be living with a 200 pound six-year-old?" Her friend snapped back. "Hey, let's go to the diner," she suggested.

"But that old guy might be there, and he might think I am interested if I show up two days in a row," Elena explained.

"Really, Elena, men don't connect the dots that well, and anyway, I am the one who is interested," Beth said.

One hour later, the two women sat innocently in the diner. Beth insisted on sitting at the same table in the corner where Elena had seen Wayne the day before. It wasn't long before Elena started and looked suddenly toward the door.

"There he is," she whispered to her friend. "Wait until I tell you where his is sitting before you start staring at him," she advised.

Beth lowered her face toward her food and sat silently. Elena could feel her heart pound as Wayne sat two tables down from them within easy hearing distance. He had noticed the turquoise hair and tall figure of the woman sitting near the window. A friend with orange hair sat across the table from her.

"They must be from the south side of Greeneville," he thought as he took a quick look at the two women. "I would say the blue-haired one must be about 32 and the other one is about 40," he thought. "I rarely see the unattractive types with the pretty ones," he concluded.

Seeing pretty women, especially those under 40, always cheered Wayne up. He was a dedicated people watcher, and he preferred females. He ordered a barbecue sandwich and vegetable soup and sat while he reflected on how attractive these two were.

Suddenly, Beth took a cigarette out of her purse. She leaned toward Wayne and loudly enough for him to hear and looking straight into his face said: "hey, baby, can you give me a light?"

Wayne looked over toward Beth and his face brightened. He stood and took a BIC lighter our of his pocket. Approaching Beth, he managed to get a look at Elena. She had pale blue eyes and he could see the light brown color of her eyelashes. He looked over at Beth. She was shorter than Elena, who was tall and slender. Beth was buxom and curvaceous with wavy hair and large green eyes.

"My name is Wayne," he said quietly as he leaned over and started a flame on the BIC lighter.

"I'm Beth and she's Elena," Beth said.

Then Beth looked straight into his eyes, parting her lips slightly and moistening them with the tip of her tongue as she held out her cigarette. She knew from experience that moistening her lips was a turn-on for some men.

"Anytime I need a light, I am coming for you," she said provocatively.

The older man felt a bit taken back by Beth's forwardness. He excused himself once he saw the cigarette take flame and he sat back down in his seat.

Wayne remained in his seat for an appropriate time, while the two women compared notes on him. Then, he left the diner. As he turned to go out the door, he looked back and Beth waved to him. He smiled and waved back. Driving home to his bungalow, he inspected the mountains outside of town. At this time of the year, the hills were still blue-green. In another month the leaves would fall. They would fall first on the mountain top where the temperature was cooler. Then, as the days of Autumn wore on, the falling leaves would work their way down the mountainside until in October, all the trees would be bare. As he unlocked the front door and walked toward the kitchen, he saw that Shelley was up.

"I have been at the diner people watching," he told his wife while sitting down in an easy chair.

"Anything going on there?" She asked.

"There were these two 30 or 40 something women. One of them asked me for a light and flirted with me a little," he replied.

"I guess they know all the men like that,' Shelley said and then smiled.

"I know that's true," he said.

Elena faintly heard Ed gritting his teeth. As she started to awaken, the sound became louder. She sat up in bed and through the dark she saw her husband laying on the side of the bed just away from her. His face was turned toward the ceiling and his features were clenched as the grinding, gritty sound of tooth against tooth continued. She was scared. Elena had been an only child. Sleeping in the same bed with someone else was unfamiliar enough. She had no grasp of what was wrong with Ed. As she leaned toward him and looked into his face, she saw that his eyes were wide open with the lids drawn back. "Ed, what's wrong?" She whispered. Ed didn't respond and she got the impression that even though his eyes were open, he didn't recognize her. She didn't have the courage to touch her husband, but slowly crawled out of bed, and dressed. She took the car keys and went out to her car. From there, she drove to her parent's house a few miles away.

Jeff and Sally awoke at one a.m. in the morning to someone knocking loudly at their door. The both sat up in bed listening to the noise outside.

"Should I call the police?" The minister whispered to his wife.

"No, it might be the neighbors in trouble. Take the shotgun and see who it is," she replied.

In his pajamas and with a twelve-gauge shotgun under his arm, the Baptist minister slowly opened the front door to see his daughter standing in the night. When Elena saw her father's face she quickly spoke.

"Dad, let me in. I'm not going back to Ed in that house," she said.

Her father, without questioning her, led her into the kitchen and they sat down to talk.

"I haven't told you and mom what Ed is like, but things have been pretty bad for the past six weeks," she said.

"What has he done?" Jeff asked.

Elena looked up into her father's face and said, "he's crazy mean."

Then she related how she had awoken and the state in which she had found her husband.

"You don't have to go back, Elena," Jeff said. "Stay with us. I will call Tom tomorrow and we will go over tomorrow and search your house," he finished.

The next morning the two elderly men forcibly entered Ed and Elena's house to find the young husband gone.

At noon on the local radio station, during the news, Jeff heard that his son-in-law was in the county jail. The radio announcer revealed that Ed McMaster had been stopped for erratic driving at five a.m. on Highway 11E, and that he had tested positive for phencyclidine. The Baptist minister then called his family attorney and made an appointment. The next day, across from the county courthouse, Elena began to fill out the paperwork to divorce Ed. Jeff paid all the attorney's fees and in time, the divorce was finalized.

Tortillas had been selling out at Pablo and Rosa's grocery. Elena was having a hard time keeping the shelves stocked. The white tortillas were a favorite of the customers. The Sanchez' always had extra whole-wheat tortillas stacked in the back of the store room. Like all family businesses, the grocery was small, but sales were sufficient to support the two parents and their three children. Their little daughter, Maria, was always scurrying about the aisles. Rosa helped Elena with stocking and the two women manned the cash register as well. Pablo and his sons, ages ten and twelve, unloaded the trucks.

It had been a while since Beth and Elena had seen Wayne at the diner. Elena had been too busy with work, and Otis had been sick. One Friday night Pablo and Rosa invited Elena to a Mexican festival in the county. Most of the migrant workers from the tomato fields by the Holston River would be there. When Pablo, Rosa and Elena had arrived, the Mariachi band was playing. Hispanic girls in colorful, long skirts performed folk dances native to Central America. By the appearance of the girls, they were of mixed Spanish and Mayan origin. The Mexican men stood and watched, clapping their hands as the band played and the dancing proceeded throughout the evening.

At the time the Sanchez' and Elena had arrived, Wayne had already been at the festival for about one hour. He had invited his wife, Shelley to go with him. Shelley didn't like crowds and had elected to stay at home watching the evening news. About ten o'clock Elena was at the taco stand ordering chicken fajitas and refried beans.

She looked to her side to see Wayne at the same stand with a
paper plate of tamales. Gathering her courage, she tapped Wayne
on the shoulder and turned toward him.

"You may not remember me, but my friend and I spoke to you at
the Market Street Diner a few weeks ago.

Wayne replied, "I was not sure what to make of your friend with the
orange hair."

Elena smiled and said, "she likes nice older men."

"What does she do?" Wayne asked.

"Beth is a nurse at the medical center and a part-time singer at the
clubs downtown," Elena replied.

"Why don't you two girls meet me at the diner, and we can get better acquainted?" The older man suggested.

Elena began to feel agitated.

"Wayne is nice, but what is really behind this invitation from a married man?" She wondered. "Well," she hesitated, searching for
a reason not to meet him, "we might be there again Saturday at
noon," she said.

When Elena called Beth to invite her to meet Wayne Saturday, Beth
did not share her friend's hesitation. On Saturday, Elena picked
Beth up in the sedan and they drove to the Market Street Diner
together. When Elena saw how Beth was dressed she felt angry.
Beth had blue sparkle eyeliner about her green eyes, and she was
wearing pink lipstick. She had squeezed into a body-hugging black
bodice and tight, faded Levi jeans. As Wayne sat down with them
and ordered, Elena assumed a stiff posture.

"We really can't stay long and talk Wayne. You understand that
don't you?" Elena explained.

"Yes, I understand. If you two have somewhere to go, that's okay," Wayne responded. "Tell me about yourselves," the older man opened the conversation.

Elena began. "I have to tell you Wayne, that I have a steady boy-friend and that I have been seeing him for over two years," she lied shamelessly.

"Yes, and as you both know, I am married," Wayne replied.

Beth tried to speak, but her friend suddenly blurted out, "and you should know that I am a regular church-going girl and that my father is a Missionary Baptist minister."

Beth broke into her friend's performance and in a comforting voice said to Wayne, "I am sorry for this honey...I was hoping that we could have a nice time."

Beth then reached out and put her hand on Wayne's forearm. Wayne scooted his chair back and stood up.

"It's been nice girls. I knew you couldn't talk long," and he turned and left.

Driving home from the diner, Beth refused to speak to Elena. The nurse and part-time singer gripped her purse and stared out the dirty windows of the car. By the time they arrived at Beth's apart-ment, Elena had hoped that her friend would come to her senses and realize that it was better not to get too close to this man-a man they hardly knew. Once Elena arrived home, her phone rang loud-ly.

"What the hell did you think you were doing at the diner?" The de-mand came over the line.

"You are too upset to talk right now," Elena snapped back.

Then she heard Beth start to cry and her friend's voice shook. "How long has it been, Elena, since a lovely man, who only needs our company, has asked either of us out?" Her friend managed to say through her tears.

"Don't lecture me, sister," Elena replied.

Then Beth hung up.

After Beth hung up, Elena took two Valium and went to bed. The sedatives did their work. The lonely woman slept through the pain of her past and the unhappiness of her present. The realization that she needed something more than a girlfriend and a cat did not make it into her dreams. When she woke Sunday afternoon, she still felt drugged by the high dose of Valium.

"If I were a drinking woman, I'd get smashed right now," she thought as she listened to Otis purring. "Instead, I guess I'll just be miserable," she reflected. Her thoughts then went back to her behavior at the diner. "Is it possible that Wayne is not like Jim, the hapless detective who was always trying to intrude on her life?" She pondered. "It doesn't matter what kind of man Wayne is: sweet and kind, or a sneaky user," she thought to herself. "I have already ended things."

While Elena was sleeping off her depression in a fog of Valium, Beth was awake. Beth had spent the night crying. At three a.m. she rose from the twisted blankets on her bed and went to look at herself in the mirror. She saw a 40 year-old woman, no longer youthful. Despite all the care she had taken earlier getting ready to meet Wayne, her hair was now disheveled, and tears created black streaks of mascara down her cheeks. At the jazz club, Beth chose to sing torch songs. Her voice was expressive and the music conveyed the struggle of women like her trying to find meaning and love in an unkind world. Right now, she despised Elena. She pondered ways she could punish her best friend for crushing her hope for the gentle compassion she had recognized in Wayne's eyes. Hanging her head, she knew that revenge on Elena would not be wise.

"I just have to move on past this," she thought to herself.

Returning to her bed, she lay awake reflecting on the kind of men she knew. They were as disjointed and lost as she was. Most of them worked in low-paying manual labor. Divorce was common and Beth was leery of getting involved with them. The fighting and swearing that poverty creates would make her more unhappy living with them than she was now.

At dawn, not having slept, she rose to get ready for her day job at the medical center. Beth was a nurse on the Orthopedic floor. The patients were like family to her. Later that day, she dropped off pain medication for an elderly woman recovering from hip surgery, the woman's son cornered her at the nurse's station.

"How long do you think my mother will be in this place?" He asked.

"At least a week, honey," she answered.

Moments later, the alarm light lit up outside the doors to three of her patient's rooms. As she administered more Lortab to one elderly man with an ankle fracture, the surgeon walked in.

"How is the patient today?" He asked.

"I hurt like hell Doc," the man answered.

"You know you need to get up and walk," the M.D. replied.

"This blow bottle you gave me to blow into is a bitch," the patient complained. "How do you expect me to get the plastic balls to the top of the bottle with my emphysema?" The patient asked.

"I don't care how you do it," the doctor emphasized, "that is, if you want to get out of this place anytime soon," he said.

"Let me get his temperature," Beth said as she leaned against the M.D. with her side, nudging him away from the patient's bedside.

"Can you take this thing out of my mouth?" The man asked.

"One hundred and two degrees Elwood," she read from the ther-
mometer, taking it out of his mouth. "Put this bottle in your mouth
and blow," she ordered.

Elwood frowned as Beth patted his hand. Dutifully, he put the blow
bottle into his mouth and began to puff.

On this day the nurse manager had convinced Beth to work a
double shift. It was early the next morning when she was finally
relieved and made plans to drive back to her apartment. The parking garage was eerily silent at this time of the morning. The garage
was never kept clean by the hospital management. Oil and grease
stains colored the bare concrete floors. To save money, the medical center had never bothered to paint the garage.

"The steel gray of the concrete floor is just ugly," she thought as she
approached her car.

Paper bags thrown onto the floor with half-eaten hamburgers inside
created litter in the corners. As her car exited the ground floor of
the parking garage, a security light threw a harsh yellow light onto
the surroundings. Beth then drove slowly through downtown. A
number of thin men with unkempt beards and long hair lay on the
city sidewalks on soiled blankets. Once she had arrived at her
apartment outside of town, she fell asleep for the first time in 48
hours.

Elena had been avoiding calling Beth.

"It has been two weeks since she chewed me out and hung up on
me," she reflected as she emptied a can of soup into a pan sitting
on the surface of her gas range.

Her parents had dropped by earlier from the outskirts of Greeneville.

"Where is your Bible?" Her father had queried as he looked around his daughter's apartment.

"I had to lend it to Beth," Elena lied. "She's been attending nightly Bible study at the Presbyterian church and needed a good study Bible," the young woman explained.

"You know, Elena, your father is conducting a revival at the county Baptist church. Why don't you come with us?" Her mother asked.

"I would but Otis is sick, and he has been throwing up all over this place. I couldn't leave him alone right now," Elena responded. "Dr. Bostick says it's allergies," she explained. "Look at the pills Otis has to take," and she shoved two large bottles into her mother's hands.

Elena knew her mother had a soft spot for Otis. Sally had given Elena the cat once he had been weaned from his mother as a kitten. Rising to leave, her parents walked toward the apartment door and her mother threw her arms around her daughter.

"You are always in our prayers, Elena," and her mother dabbed her moist eyes.

Elena looked at the phone once her parents had left. She was afraid to call her friend, but decided she couldn't abandon Beth even if she had been the cause of Beth's unhappiness. After a few rings, the nurse answered the phone.

"I guess you had to call eventually, didn't you?" Beth said, recognizing the caller ID.

"How are things at the hospital?" The grocery clerk asked.

"At least on the Ortho floor, there are people to talk to," Beth answered. "You know, Elena," she continued, "I have been to the diner several times and I haven't seen Wayne," Beth said.

"He's probably realized he's not going to get any action, if you know what I mean," Elena explained.

"It may come as a surprise to you, sister, but there really are some decent men in this town," Beth said. "I guess they all seem to miss you," she concluded.

"Beth, I am sorry about Wayne. I just felt I had to set him straight on where I am coming from," Elena explained.

"The next nice guy we meet, you keep your trap shut, okay?" Beth demanded.

Over the years, happiness had managed to elude Elena. She had been painfully shy in high school and had not dated much. Her ex-husband, Ed, had been an actual disaster. To compensate, Elena had developed a fantasy lover-Frank. Something of a hopeless romantic, this tall, shy beauty had been dreaming about Frank for years. As she sat on the couch in the darkness of her apartment, she could hear Frank knocking at the door. Elena opened the door as usual. She was amazed at how incredibly good-looking her Frank was.

"I'll never know why he picked me," she thought with satisfaction as he planted a big kiss on her waiting lips.

"I have tickets to the show at Freedom Hall," he said with glee, seeing the sparkle in her eyes.

"Oh, Franky, how did you know that I was dying to go," she gushed.

As Frank walked Elena from her apartment to his car, he reached out and took her hand. Elena squeezed his fingers teasingly as she looked over at him. Always the gentleman, he carefully held the door to his BMW open as she slipped inside into the leather seat.

"Mother and Dad are in the Bahamas until next Thursday," he mentioned as he ran his fingers across her arm.

Breathless, Elena smiled and looked straight ahead, her eyes blinking nervously.

"Otis likes you Franky," she said softly. The shiny car sped down the highway toward Freedom Hall.

Maria began screaming and tugging at Elena's skirt. Elena looked down to see the little girl grab a package of noodles.

"Rosa, can you do something with her?" The clerk asked in a high nervous voice.

"Here little one, you like this?" The mother pleaded as she held out a package of candy corn.

Maria grabbed the orange and yellow candy from the package and began pushing the candy into her mouth. Rosa took a wet rag out of her oversized skirt and began forcibly wiping her daughter's cheeks. She struggled to hold Maria in place and continued cleaning her face.

"Someday, I will have a little girl like Maria," Elena said to Rosa.

"You gotta find a good man, honey," Rosa replied. "How you gonna get a good husband working in Sanchez grocery and sitting alone in you little apartment?" The Mexican woman continued.

Without answering, Elena returned to stacking the packages of noodles.

Elena had lived in Greeneville her entire life. She rarely traveled beyond the limits of the small Southern town. In her 32 years, she had come to know the male population of Greeneville intimately.

Settling down was expensive and stressful. Men found that life was better playing the field of lonely women, and dumping any of them who became too serious or demanding.

There was desperate competition among the girls for the few men who could afford a wife and family, and there weren't many of the hard-working and serious type in Greeneville. Some girls thought of moving away to Knoxville where there were more single and successful men. Most girls, however, being from the rural South, felt that moving away from home was frightening. Knoxville was over 100 miles away, and if they couldn't land a big fish quickly, life there would be incredibly lonely.

There were two men in Elena's life who seemed to be the kind of man that she needed: her father Jeff, and Rosa's husband, Pablo. Of these two men, she was around Pablo more frequently. He worked the small Latino grocery with his wife and family. Being Hispanic, the Sanchez' were Catholic and very family oriented. Not only did Pablo and Rosa have three fine children, but they had a passel of relatives back in Juarez. All the Sanchez family were short in stature. The father, though, had a muscular chest and stout legs. He could work any man in Greenevile under the table in Elena's estimation. And Pablo never looked at other women. There were many single women who frequented the grocery for tortillas and salsa, and he was always polite and respectful with them.

Three months after Wayne tried to have lunch with Beth and Elena, loneliness drove the pair of friends to attend the local Missionary Baptist Church. Both Beth and Elena had at least one nice Sunday dress. Beth was dressed in a flouncy skirt that showed her shapely legs. The skirt was a floral pattern with large blue flowers stamped into the fabric. Around her narrow waist she wore a black, metal belt with an attractive silver clasp in front. As was usual, Beth meant to attract attention. She had spent most of her week's salary on the cosmetics with which she was made up.

Elena, on the other hand, was an example of female modesty.

And she did have a reputation to uphold. After all, her father had spent an entire week preaching here. She wore a cream-colored calf-length dress with tiny yellow polka dots. Her turquoise hair was pulled back and up into a bun on the top of her head with a pretty ivory pin to keep her hair in place. During the service, Elena couldn't help but notice the married men with their wives and families. When she saw the women scold their noisy children during the sermon, she found herself possessed with wonder. She struggled to understand where the couples had met and become introduced to one another. In her experience, if you didn't meet Mr. Right by chance, you didn't meet him at all. The only place she knew for singles were the lewd bars on the county line. To her, an atmosphere of disrepute pervaded the air of these places.

Beth had just finished her first set of songs. Her voice was in good shape tonight, but she had been concerned about the smoke in the room. Cigarettes were bad for the vocal cords. The crowd had been appreciative and the tips in the bucket at the front of the stage had been good. As she walked through the crowd toward the bar, she felt a hand reach out. Turning, she saw a nicely dressed man at a table near the aisle. He was sitting with a young blonde female, but the presence of the woman did not prevent him from approaching Beth.

"My wife and I would like to meet you," the man said looking up at her.

"I do have some free time before my next set. Would you buy me a drink?" She asked.

The man smiled and stood up, helping Beth into a chair. He had an odd look about him. She couldn't decide what was different about him, but his smile just seemed a bit strange. The young blonde grasped her drink with both hands in front of her on the table.

"I'll have a cherry spritzer," Beth said, affecting her most engaging smile as she looked at the couple.

"Where did you learn to sing like this?" The man asked.

"I started singing at school in the chorus when I was twelve," Beth answered.

"By the way, my name is Jonathan, and this is my wife, Sue," he interjected.

"I am Beth, the singer said.

"What do you do when you are not singing in this club? We haven't seen you before," Jonathan said.

"I am a regular down the street," Beth answered. "This gig is just a filler for right now. My regular club wanted to try out a new girl, and they gave me the night off," she continued.

"Can you dance?" Sue asked, looking at Beth.

"I am not much on the dance floor," Beth said, not knowing where the two were headed with the conversation.

Beth looked up at Bob, the bouncer, who was a pretty big and intimidating guy. Bob came over and tapped Jonathan on the shoulder.

"Hey, buddy. She needs to go," he said.

"Wait a minute," Jonathan said loudly: "I'm having a talk with the lady."

"You've had your talk from what I can see," Bob said.

"You can't talk to him that way!" Sue shouted.

Beth put down her cherry spritzer on the table and began to get out of her chair.

"I really need to go," she said in a forced undertone, and she headed with Bob back to the bar.

Once back at the bar with Bob, Beth asked the people around her, "anyone know that guy I was sitting with?"

An older man with short gray hair in a blue suit spoke: "he is president of the Bank of Greeneville, Jonathan Carpenter."

"His wife looks kinda young, if you ask me," Beth said.

The man in the blue suit turned to the bartender. "Stephanie, give me a whisky sour." Then he leaned down and whispered: "she's not his wife."

"Is he married then?" Beth asked.

"Oh, yes, everyone in Greeneville knows Cindy Carpenter, but the woman over there is not Cindy," the man said.

Looking back at the table, Jonathan and Sue had returned to their drinks, and were watching the dancers on the floor.

Beth looked up at Bob, "just think Bobby, I coulda made it to the big time," she said and she twirled a whisp of hair in her fingers.

Later, after Beth had finished her second set of songs and was picking up her purse to go, she felt a hand on her behind. She looked around and was startled to see Jonathan and Sue. She tried to see where Jonathan's hands were, but the wide smile on his face caught her attention.

"Don't tell me you didn't like that?" Sue said looking straight into Beth's eyes.

Beth was speechless, and turned her back on them. She walked quickly toward the door, only to find Jonathan walking beside her.

"Hey, honey," he raised his voice as he grabbed Beth's arm, "my wife and I are looking for another place to go tonight. How about it?" The broad smile spread across his face again.

Beth panicked and pushed him to the side of the aisle as she hurried toward the exit.

"Why that whore!" Sue hissed.

Within minutes, Beth was out in the parking lot. Not daring to go to her car, she walked across the street and stood on the asphalt behind an old liquor store. Taking out her cell phone, she waited until Jonathan and Sue had left Tony's. She peeked around the side of the liquor store building. The bright neon light at Tony's was turned off and the street was deserted.

Frank and Elena sat on the couch watching movies. Otis jumped onto Elena's lap, knocking the bowl of popcorn on its side.

"I can get it, honey," Frank said as he stood to gather the popcorn. Elena's attention was on the movie.

The hero had just rescued the heroine from poverty and married her. It was a Cinderella story. Frank had given her the portable television set. The gift was to celebrate their first anniversary together.

"I have nothing to give you in return, Franky," she had blubbered as she unwrapped the gift.

Her boyfriend leaned down and kissed her on the top of her head. "You have no idea what you have already given me," he said.

At the end of the movie, Elena walked her beau to the door. "I'll be seeing you soon," Frank said as he threw his arms around her. The young girl was in heaven.

Elena picked up her cell phone and made a call.

"Girl, I have been waiting for you to call," Beth answered.

Still shaken from her experience at Tony's a few nights before, Beth was in need of a diversion.

"How has it been in the grocery business?" The nurse asked.

"The wholesale truck had a flat tire and couldn't make the weekly delivery," Elena explained. "Pablo is hopping mad, He and his two sons are making the runs to Knoxville in the pickup. It's been a real test for the tires of the old truck," she said.

"Say, Elena, do you have time for a trip to Goodwill?" Beth asked. "I am in need of few things," she said. "It's getting hot in this apartment."

"I can be at Goodwill in 20 minutes," Elena answered.

At Goodwill, Beth rummaged through the blouses and dresses. Elena noticed that her friend had not put on makeup that day. Beth's lightly freckled face was stern. "I saw Jim at the diner," she mentioned holding up a blouse with a ruffle neckline.

"He was there the other evening while I was having chicken nuggets," Elena complained. "The guy looks pretty bad," Elena continued. "I would guess he has put on 15 pounds," she said.

"Tell him to give up beer," Beth advised.

"Giving up beer and women both would benefit that guy," Elena responded. "You know, he kept whining about my not going out with him," she continued. "He's the last thing I need right now. As if I need a man to keep me happy," she finished.

As the two women finished shopping at Goodwill, Beth's mind reverted to Wayne. "Here was a man with something to offer," she thought to herself.

"He's taken though," she pondered.

She had seen him at the diner a few weeks before, but he had avoided looking at her. Taking advantage of his reticence, she had given him a real look-over. As Elena had related a few months before, although he was older, he was exceedingly good looking. He had kept his wavy hair and he had not developed the large stomach that most of the men his age had. And he was quiet and well-mannered.

"A real gentleman," she thought.

Elena and Beth paid for their purchases and walked out of Goodwill.

"I am gonna meet this Wayne somehow, if it's the last thing I ever do," Beth promised herself as she got into her car.

Month after month went by. Autumn turned to Winter and Winter turned to Spring. Beth had been going to the Market Street Diner every week. Frequently, she was there alone. From time to time she managed to get Elena to go with her. The diner was her only possible connection to Wayne, and she theorized that, sooner or later, she would seen him there. Her initial hope led to despair and then to resignation. It was really hit or miss if she would ever see him again. Wayne had been avoiding the diner after his disappointment at the hands of the lovely Elena. He felt foolish, at his age, trying to get to know these two younger women.

One day, Wayne and Shelley were sitting in their kitchen.

"Wayne, honey, could you go get some of that good barbecue you used to bring home?" Shelley asked her husband.

"It really isn't good for you, Shelley," he answered.

"Could you get some, please?" She asked.

Wayne fired up the old car and drove to the diner. The diner had the best barbecue in Greeneville, as he well knew. He walked into the diner at six p.m. As far as he could tell, the place was deserted. He ordered two pounds of barbecue and sat in the corner to wait for the cook to chop up the pork and add the seasoning. On this particular evening, as Wayne sat in the corner, Beth happened to walk in. Instantly, she saw him. After all this time, here was the man she had searched for. What would happen if she just walked up to him? The comely woman with the orange hair approached tentatively and stood just behind him. She reached out and tapped him on the shoulder with her index finger. As Wayne turned around, her courage began to fail.

In a low voice, the 40 year-old woman spoke: "Please don't run away, honey. Can I just have a talk with you?" She pleaded.

"It has been a while since your friend told me off, but I guess we can talk a bit," he replied.

The nurse quickly took a seat facing Wayne and she began to regain her courage.

"I don't know if you recall me, but I'm Beth." And she held out a limp and diminutive hand.

"Yes, Beth, how could I forget you?" Wayne said, feeling a bit more comfortable and managing to smile.

"I'm a divorced nurse. I know you are married and all, but do you know hard it is to find decent male friends in Greeneville?" Beth asked.

"I can imagine Beth," he said. "I was born here in Greeneville. It has been a long time since high school for me, but life in this town has been very hard. I would guess it has been that way for you," he said.

As Wayne began to relate his experience of over 60 years in Greeneville, Beth looked up at him, eagerly taking in his manner of speaking and expressions. On his side, Wayne began to notice how nice Beth was for the first time.

"She is very pretty," Wayne thought to himself.

Her orange hair was neatly brushed. Her complexion was soft with pale freckles, and her manner was open and becoming. After the two had been introduced and learned something about one another, Beth's natural boldness came to the fore.

"Let me be frank, Wayne. I am a lonely woman, and I need a friendship with a nice older man like you. Do you think we could be friends?" She asked.

"Beth, I have wanted a friendship like this for years," he answered.

Anxious not to ruin things, the singer and nurse was determined to honor Wayne's marriage. Beth knew she had been absolutely desperate for anything other than the life she had led since she had walked out on her ex-husband.

That August it was insufferably hot in Greeneville. Elena had not heard from her friend in a while. Although she had been busy at Sanchez grocery, she had wondered how Beth was. Then, one Saturday, Beth called Elena and invited her over to watch a movie on the television at her apartment. The two women loved the same kind of movie: action adventure.

Beth and Elena had just finished a two-hour feature. Elena looked at her cell phone: ten pm.-time to go.

"Well, it has been fun Beth. We should do this more often," she said as she stood to gather her things.

Beth became quiet, looking off into the distance of the room. "Don't go right now Elena. Sit down for a while," she said.

The grocery store clerk sat back down on the couch.

"He's mine, Elena," Beth said looking straight into the room.

Elena chuckled a bit and then said, "who is yours Beth, what is this?"

"That darling man Wayne. He's mine," she repeated with conviction in her voice.

"How do you know this Beth? We haven't seen him in over a year now. Just face it; it's over with him," Elena pleaded.

"No, I have been seeing him at the diner, once per week, for quite a while," the nurse said.

Then Elena became excited, "look Beth, you know Wayne is married. You have no right to carry on with him," she said. Elena became emphatic, "you just have no right to do this!" She said.

"It's all right Elena. He has told me about the limits to our relationship, and about his wife Shelley," Beth said calmly.

"Then why hang around this guy? You need to move on," the clerk repeated.

"He loves me, Elena, and he's mine," Beth repeated.

"And how do you know Wayne loves you? What has this man told you?" Elena asked.

"Look, Elena, how sure are you that the sun will rise in the morning?" Beth asked.

"What?" Elena exclaimed.

"That is how sure I am of Wayne," Beth said and then continued, "and I can tell you this, Elena, he will never leave me. And some-day, if Shelley is gone and he is alone, Wayne will come to me. And Elena I will be here waiting."

www.ingramcontent.com/pod-product-compliance
Lightning Source LLC
Chambersburg PA
CBHW011237120626
46549CB00009B/3307